FINDING THE WORDS

Stories and Poems
of Women Veterans

Finding the Words: Stories and Poems of Women Veterans

Editor: Shari Wagner
Book Design and Layout: Andrea Boucher

ISBN: 978-0-9967438-4-6

Printed in the United States of America

INwords PUBLICATIONS
PRESENTED BY THE **INDIANA WRITERS CENTER**

Kurt Vonnegut
MEMORIAL LIBRARY

INDIANA WRITERS CENTER

ALLEN WHITEHILL CLOWES CHARITABLE FOUNDATION

INDIANA ARTS COMMISSION
MAKING THE ARTS HAPPEN

WITH SUPPORT FROM:
ARTSCOUNCIL
AND THE CITY OF INDIANAPOLIS

BUTLER | JORDAN COLLEGE
of the ARTS

Table of Contents

Introduction

The camouflage uniform Shanna Reis wore in the Army no longer hangs in her closet. She cut up the material and shaped the wet fibers into handmade paper, the same paper she used when making the poignant print on this book cover.

The following stories and poems are also part of a transformative, artistic process. Shanna and the other nine members of the Women Veterans Memoir Workshop—Leslie Bales, Robin Hall, Loc Hornung, Laura McKee, Anita Siccardi, Betty Smith, Christylee Vickers, Julia Whitehead, and Lisa Wilken—have transformed their military experiences into powerful memoirs.

To do this, they had to find the words. They had to find the words for personal experiences that sometimes seemed too complicated or embarrassing or painful for words.

And they had to find the *right* words. As Mark Twain once quipped, "The difference between the *almost right* word and the *right* word is . . . the difference between the lightning bug and the lightning."

The right words won't come if the memoir writer stays distant from her material, safe behind a façade of clichés and abstractions. Lightning strikes when a writer relives her experience as she writes about it—remembering what she heard, saw, touched, smelled, and tasted. Proximity to painful experiences can be difficult, but not finding the right words for what's stored inside is ultimately more painful. Finding the right words allows the writer to exert control and, paradoxically, discover release as memory is transformed into art.

Not only did these ten women find the right words, they found them *together*.

Before we met for our first workshop, I wondered how the veterans would get along. Would the women who had been actively deployed and the ones who had served as reservists forge connections? Would those who had found careers in the military and those who hadn't find much in common? Would differences in age, level of education, writing ability, or trauma from wartime service cause rifts?

I needn't have worried. A strong community of mutual support formed during our first workshops in October as the women wrote about why they enlisted and what they learned in basic training. Throughout the next six months, these women, whose age difference spanned as much as sixty years, discovered more common ground, especially as they recalled the camaraderie they felt during their service and what it was like being a woman in the military.

If all of these factors had not brought them together, the endeavor to find the right words would have been sufficient. When a workshop's collective goal is a published book, writing, critiquing, and editing become a collaborative process. These authors took delight in helping each other find the right words and the right strategies for organizing them. Over time, it grew increasingly clear to me that our workshop provided a sense of camaraderie akin to what the writers experienced during their time in the military. I wasn't surprised when the women made plans to continue meeting after our final workshop.

What if every veteran returning home had the opportunity to become part of an art-based workshop such as ours? Sebastian Junger in his May 7, 2015 *Vanity Fair* article, "How PTSD Became a Problem Far Beyond the Battlefield," asserts that cases of PTSD have dramatically risen because soldiers coming home from service return to a fragmented, individualistic society that cannot integrate their experiences, a society that may be "deeply brutalizing to the human spirit." He goes on to say, "A modern soldier returning from combat goes from the kind of close-knit situation that humans evolved for into a society where most people work outside the home, children are educated by strangers, families are isolated from wider communities, personal gain almost completely eclipses collective good, and people sleep alone or with a partner. Even if he or she is in a family, that is not the same as belonging to a large, self-sufficient group that shares and experiences almost everything collectively." I believe the camaraderie of art-based workshops could help alleviate feelings of isolation.

The goal of this collaborative book is to find the right words *as a gift to others.*

That last phrase is significant. This book is a gift—an offering from ten courageous women who stepped into the unknown when they enlisted and now step into the unknown as they share their very personal stories. These writers are motivated by the belief that women veteran voices have been silent for too long.

Because these veterans found the right words, you, as a reader, will step into their boots. You will discover why they enlisted and what they learned in basic training. You will travel with them through deserts, mountains, and mine-laden ground. You will watch them load cargo planes, repair engines, balance accounts, learn to load a gun, and treat the injured. You will admire them as they speak up against injustice and exert their authority. You will grieve when they are injured and when they stand in silence for funeral taps. You will rejoice when they receive letters from school children and find true love. You will root for them as they struggle with depression and advocate for the welfare of veterans.

Ultimately, like me, you will find your world enlarged by the fortitude and candor of these ten remarkable women.

Shari Wagner
Instructor and Editor
Indiana Writers Center
September 2016

There is no greater agony than bearing an untold story inside you.

Maya Angelou

Shanna Reis joined the Indiana National Guard in 2000 at seventeen years old. She served as a Specialist in the Military Police Platoon of the 76th INF BDE. She was deployed to Iraq and to Afghanistan. Her contract with the military ended in 2012.

Shanna Reis

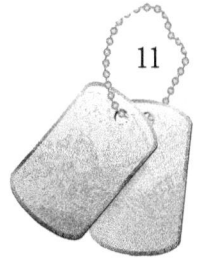

I WAS A 240B GUNNER

SHANNA REIS

Why I Enlisted

I WAS BORN INTO A military family with one member or more in each major war. My stepfather was active Navy, and I grew up moving from state to state. Until I hit sixth grade, I rarely spent more than a year in the same school. I could say my family's history in the military is why I joined, but I'd be lying. That legacy is important to me and my family, but it is not why I chose to enlist.

In high school, attending college was a nebulous thing for me, a far-off goal that I was expected to attain but distant even in my senior year in 2000. I rarely thought about college as anything more than another four years of school. Doing what? I sure didn't know at the time, but I would be doing something there.

I knew my family could afford to send me through college and that I could even consider grants and loans to help offset some of the cost. Money would work itself out, and I had no real need to worry about it. Still, I listened to the recruiter that came to state his pitch: Join the National Guard. Work for your community, be part of something bigger, and get your tuition paid. It sounded great to me. What did I know about the National Guard anyway? They always showed up when floods happened and threw sandbags around. Six years of one weekend a month and two weeks in the summer didn't sound like a bad tradeoff for a college degree. After all, I had a younger sister and brother; the money saved on me could be put aside for them when they were old enough for college.

So I signed up. I didn't think about my family who had been or still were in various branches. Thoughts of them did not factor into my decision at all, really, except, maybe for all of five seconds, as a feeling that signing up was a normal thing for people to do.

I talked to a family friend who was a recruiter and let her take the credit for my enlistment. I filled out a ton of paperwork, went through the physical, got sworn in, and even sat down with my mom to sign emancipation forms. At seventeen I was legally a minor and wouldn't be old enough to sign without parental permission until the end of boot camp.

My mom asked me once if this was what I wanted and then signed the papers with me. We never really talked about my enlistment. No one mentioned anything while I was joining up. Even with the paperwork filed to legally declare me as an adult, I did not think about any of it except as another step. Boot camp was far off—one week after I got my diploma—and just one more step to take before college.

I took the split option. I would go through boot and then get a year off to attend college. Then I'd go right back to complete AIT, my actual job training, the next summer. I thought it was a neat little plan.

I was introduced to my unit six months before boot camp. They had a platoon set aside for non-priors, the people who had no previous military experience or training. There were a lot of people joining up at the time who were assigned to units but had training dates months away. We were kept aside from the company and given to a sergeant close to retiring. His favorite thing to do was to make us march around like a drunken caterpillar and then hide us away in the weed-filled, unused parts of the motor pool. We were a mismatched group of people in civilian clothes whose reasons for being there ranged from the need for college money to an alternative for time in jail (if one guy was to be believed). We rarely interacted with anyone else in the unit.

I went through six drills of that before I graduated. Then I had a week to finish paperwork for college before packing for training. They gave me a list of things to bring, and I spent my last night at home wondering what they meant by *calf-length socks*. What part of the calf did they need the socks to end at? Was mid-calf acceptable or did they need the whole calf covered? I ended up buying a package of men's socks that went all the way up to my knee just to be safe. The time I spent in the store deciding on socks was longer than the time I'd spent on my decision to enlist.

I wasn't thinking about why I joined or what I wanted when I flew out to get bussed to Fort Leonard Wood. Didn't think about it as I went through an assembly line of clothing, more paperwork, and way too many needles. Not at all as I was herded onto a cattle truck, standing-room-only, and taken to the barracks. Not one single thought in my head at all until the truck doors opened and the drill sergeants descended.

As I listened to the barked and purposely confusing commands, I think I had my first real thought since I had first signed my name on that line: *Oh, shit, what did I do?*

It's been fifteen years since that moment, and, aside from some truly spectacularly hot training weeks in summer, I have not regretted where the decision to join has led me, though I'd really like to go back in time and smack my younger self in the head. College tuition sounds fine and dandy as far as reasons go, but it doesn't sit right with me these days. It took me almost fourteen years to get the damn college degree that started me on my course. I mostly got it just because I thought it was stupid to go through all that I've been through and not get what I wanted in the first place. I'll keep telling people who ask that's the reason because it sounds a lot better than the truth I stumbled across that first day at boot camp.

I joined up because I wasn't thinking.

Split Option

I USED THE SPLIT OPTION when joining up because it sounded reasonable to me. I'd go through boot camp one summer, take two semesters off for college, and then go back for another summer of training focused on my job as an MP, Military Police. To a teenage kid, not having to wait to start college sounded like an *awesome* idea, but it was more of me just not thinking at all. It was probably the worst decision I could have made.

Boot camp itself seemed to go on forever, but I cannot give a linear account of it. I can't even remember the people I trained with anymore because I kept to myself as much as possible. I don't think I've seen anyone from boot camp since 2000. I have more memories of the people I went to AIT (Advanced Individual Training) with the following year. The days were filled with classes and lessons, but hell if I can remember any specific part of it now. Some of the training has stuck with me as words, but most of it has become instinctual.

The lessons I do remember are these:

I learned that simply breathing can be painful when your body is being broken down and remolded into something with more muscle than a 110 pound girl can dream of having. That nothing in the Army can ever be clean enough, and it's easier to just not stop cleaning if you don't want to be in trouble. I learned that every meal can be eaten faster between two slices of bread, and tasting while eating only wastes the precious seconds you're allowed to eat. I learned it's impossible to overdose on vitamin C drops and that digging your nails in your scalp can keep you awake.

I learned that I can get hungry enough to want to eat a squirrel raw. That sometimes faking sleep while a drill sergeant is yelling at your bunkmate at 2 a.m. is the only sane option available to you. That being naked in a crowded shower isn't awkward or embarrassing unless you let it be so. I discovered that there are people stupid enough to try to overdose on aspirin and people stupid enough to tear their muscles trying to max out their scores during the Physical Training test.

I learned that sometimes it hurts more to stop than it does to press on, and it is possible to get blisters *inside* of other blisters. That if you tuck each layer of sheets and blankets into each individual spring under the mattress it's almost impossible for your bunk to be flipped over. I learned that volunteering meant you couldn't complain and that I should never volunteer for anything ever again in my life. I also found out that "voluntold" is a word to be dreaded.

I learned to fear a drill sergeant who is absolutely silent, but not as much as one that is smiling. That poison ivy exists and simply clearing it off the ground won't stop you from getting it all over your legs. I found out that candy tasting like shampoo can seem like manna. Also, that chaplains can be evil pranksters if they want to be.

Most importantly of all, from my point of view at least, I learned that I cannot run fast.

I was awesome at doing push-ups and could easily score points for them. Sit-ups were a pain I could manage with a moderate amount of effort. Both of these exercises are in the Army trifecta, that is the Physical Training test—PT for those without the breath to say that mouthful. Running, though, is the third part of the test and just about killed me.

Sure, I can run. It isn't physically impossible for me to do. I can even run long distances, if needed, with only moderate complaining. What I cannot do is run fast. I could not make the two-mile run in the time needed to pass the test they periodically gave us during training, not easily at least. I eventually managed to pass it for boot camp—but barely, on the very last test they gave.

Run days were the days I dreaded most in training, and since they happened every other day, I never got much of a break from them. I always came in last, too. I was either the one the run group would be forced to circle back around to pick up or the one who was last to cross the line during the tests. In boot camp I had a horrible case of shin splints pretty much the whole time and annoying hairline fractures in both feet that persisted in causing me pain for six months afterwards. Because I used the pain as an excuse not to keep up with my running, my dread/hate cycle of run days repeated themselves all over again when AIT came around in 2001.

It got so bad that some nights all I'd dream about was running. Not just running, but the whole lead up to going out for a run. While I slept, dread made me restless.

Running was not, and still is not, a thing I do well, which makes the fact that I was in the military weirdly funny to some people. My hatred of running, however, is just one reason why I grew to love the job I chose so much in the end: 95B, Military Police, field MPs; *death before dismount.*

Why run when you have a perfectly good vehicle to drive in? That might be said as a joke by others, but every time I said it, I *meant* it. If I needed to run away, my chances of survival on foot were much worse than in any vehicle. And if I had to chase anyone? Well, there's a reason I refused to give up my position as a gunner. I never met anyone that could outrun seven hundred to nine hundred rounds per minute.

I never once needed to run during my time in the Army anyway. Not even when I was deployed and our policy of "death before dismount" was tested. I still have nightmares about running though. They're second only to my dreams where I'm packing my bags and waiting around to deploy again. It's a little depressing that the run days are probably the clearest memories I have of training.

The Myth of Front Lines

MY UNIT WAS MOBILIZING FOR deployment to Iraq about mid-2008, I think. Timeframes are a little hazy for me, especially when it comes to the massive pre-deployment song and dance everyone has to go through. There's a huge checklist of training and tests that must be completed before a soldier can deploy, an entire book of needed signatures so that later, if problems arise, those in command can say, "No, that soldier received the proper training. Look, here's his signature saying he completed it. It's not our fault he did something stupid."

That's a cynical thought, maybe, but my company was halfway through that damn checklist when the signatures we had accumulated were lost and we were made to do everything all over again, from the beginning. Being cynical and sarcastic was really all that kept us sane as we went through the same death-by-PowerPoint training slides again. Did we really need to go through slides on proper hand sanitization twice?

My platoon's mission changed as the pre-deployment went on, and we ended up getting more training than we needed. We weren't complaining, though, because it's not every day that you get offered the military equivalent of SWAT training and the opportunity to shoot a lot without having to worry about qualifying.

The up side to all the training was that by the time we were shipped to Fort Stewart in Georgia for our final tasks, we were acting like a mostly well-oiled machine, a little creaky still, but functioning at top shape. We all knew our roles in the platoon even though the final configurations of the three-man teams were left up in the air until we reached Stewart.

I was a 240B gunner. For years I'd always been thrown the 249 SAW, and I was good with it, so my position with the 240 was a sure thing. When my team was finalized, I was working with a driver and team leader I'd known since I first joined. Most of our training at Stewart consisted of the platoon driving in our teams and reacting to a stopped convoy, suspicious trash, or a dozen other things that never really applied to reality. A few training lanes even allowed us to drive and shoot actual bullets instead of blanks, as long as we faced only one way and didn't drive too fast.

It was good practice in some ways, though. It got to the point where we knew how every team would react to just about any situation before anything happened, and that's the kind of knowledge that saves people.

During one of the training missions, we were approached by a couple of people from public affairs. They were taking photos for various reasons and wanted pictures of a gunner for a recruitment poster. They didn't choose me, but instead asked the only other female gunner in the platoon.

It only took about twenty or so minutes for them to get a few pictures of her in the turret behind her weapon. With her eyes focused on a faraway spot, she looked perfectly alert and ready to engage. The PR people promised to send copies and then left shortly afterwards to take more pictures somewhere else. We all teased this gunner about having her face on a poster, and then we forgot all about it until weeks later.

We were already in Iraq then and had completed the changeover with the unit we were replacing. We had trailers for rooms and controlled our own office, our own mission-ready vehicles, and a few connexes full of gear we'd mostly finished inventorying and organizing. The other gunner received an email with the publicity pictures and an explanation that she shared with the platoon.

The pictures looked great. Despite the rather obvious yellow blank adapter on the end of her weapon, she looked like a badass gunner ready to go out and unload everything she had on anything that moved. The story that came with the pictures was not so great. The recruitment poster was nixed after debate from people higher up. It was not to be used in any capacity. Why? Because no one wanted to give the American public the impression that women were being used in a combat role. The pictures were deemed too controversial.

In Iraq we had four women in our platoon. Two of us were drivers, and two of us were gunners. No one seemed to bat an eye at the drivers, though some guys never failed to make the old cracks about women drivers. Mention us two gunners, though? There were more than a few long pauses and squinty looks.

In a convoy the gunner position is the most exposed. We were taught to keep as low a profile as possible while up there, but we still had to scan for any threats or obstacles. If we were attacked, the gunner had a high chance of injury, and if the vehicle rolled, it was more often than not an accepted fact that the gunner would get seriously hurt or die. Some people couldn't understand why a woman would be in that position.

I think our lieutenant faced some questioning about that, though he never really shared it with the rest of us. In his platoon the positions in the vehicle went to those who could handle them best. The gunners were those of us who did best with our weapons and could handle being up in the turret. Rank and gender didn't come into consideration for that much. It was the lieutenant's policy to place people in spots where they'd proven to do well in the past. It was strange to me that there were people who wouldn't think like that, too.

While I was in Iraq, I knew there was this free-floating myth in the U.S. that women weren't allowed on the front lines. It was vaguely acknowledged and talked about in the media and a joke tossed around in the ranks. The fact was, in both my deployments, I never once saw a front line of any kind, which is why I laughed when I heard about women on the front lines. Sure, there were no women on the front lines, but where exactly was this mythical line everyone was so concerned about? The threat was all around, and the enemy could hit anywhere regardless of the imaginary line people back home were so worried about.

It exasperates me how people are still debating this today—whether women should or should not be on a line that doesn't exist. That there's a debate about women in combat years and even decades after the fact that women have already been involved in combat is ridiculous. Some of the people arguing against it seem determined to deny the existence of those women who have engaged in combat, the men who worked with those women just as efficiently as with each other, and the accomplishments these mixed-forces attained.

They say women don't fight,
On front lines that don't exist.

They say women don't fight,
In a war that never ends.

They say women don't fight,
In countries where *safe* is a myth.

They say women don't fight,
And I say bullshit♥

Boots on Ground

My tan boots are
blackened from wear.
Afghanistan is caked
into the boot strings.
Iraq is ground dark
into the toes and heel.
And my homeland is just
a trace on the sole.

GIB—Guy In Back

I opted out of the sightseeing
For an extra 30 minutes of sleep,
Precious as gold. I was irritated
At losing even a few of them.

Brought in to my shift early,
I did not notice the heavy air
Or the eyes that followed after me
Until the radio desk caught me.

The sticky note was orange and small.
A blank square covered an inked

Page filled with a tragedy of details
Jotted on a lined notepad.

I reached for it, wanted to turn
Over that blank square to see
The hidden letters of names underneath
But I was called away too fast.

Stacked water cases trembled close to falling.
A broken thermometer predicted 100.
I fixated on the paint peeling under the sun,
As my ears refused what I was told.

Third vehicle
Returning to camp
Land mine
They're not coming back

There was talk of flag-covered boxes.
The shine of tears in squinting eyes.
A dull ringing in my ears as
My mind insisted *it's all a joke.*

It was no joke, no laugh followed.
Inside again I lifted the note.
Surrounded by shorthand
Four names I knew.

MSR Tampa at Night

      It was blinding.
There and gone in seconds, leaving behind an afterimage of rainbow colors.
Smoke rolled into the headlight beams and slowly gave way to the Humvee in
front. The gunner's cage was ripped away and the locked door swung open on
a broken hinge.
      Burning. Heat.
Fuel. Dirt. The unmistakable scent of explosion. The smell of violence thick
with debris that coated my lungs with destruction and weighed my body

down to an endless crawl.

Dirt, sand, and shit.

A near constant taste that lingered and flavored everything as it stuck to the tongue. Carbon and CLP. The spices of life for all gunners with a working gun and the will to use it. Smoke. A rarer taste that lingered for days afterwards turning the flavor of food to ash.

The concussive wave.

It was a punch to the chest. The pressure of its rage rattled my body and left my head ringing. It rocked trucks and people even as it felt like Earth herself shook under us all.

Nothing.

Not one sound from the time the radio crackled, "Object to the right," all the way up to the broken sound of the first accidentally transmitted scream as the damaged truck kept lurching on. That much violence should have been deafening, but I remember only silence.

Home Again

IT WAS 2005, AND I was only a few weeks back from my first deployment to Afghanistan. I was on I70 East, driving two friends home from downtown Indianapolis, just entering the ramp for 465, when I had a freak out. The curve to get onto the beltway wasn't that bad, but it's a long curve that exerts some pressure on drivers. It makes your ass stick to the seat especially at the customary twenty to thirty miles above the speed limit that all Indy drivers follow.

In that long moment taking the curve, I felt like I was losing control of the vehicle, like I was going to skid out and roll over. I don't remember what I said as I let off the gas pedal, in the left-most lane to boot, but I remember what my best friend of too many years said with a laugh: "It's a curve. Oh god, get over it." She was thoroughly amused at my panic. It's been over a decade now and that comment still hurts.

To be honest, it's in line with the kind of relationship we have. Like family, we express our friendship with cutting words and sarcasm. Usually these harsh remarks are followed by real help if it's needed, but not that time. I clammed up and said nothing about it at all. It was my second incidence of overreacting.

The first freak-out had been in a store filled with too many people, so crowded I retreated to the car to sit for three hours. With no target, tension and anger filled me and left me shaken—shaken at my response to something so harmless. I realized then I wasn't as fine as I liked to say I was.

In the months that followed the ramp experience, overreaction and freaking out became more frequent. These episodes were followed by hallucinations and irrational thoughts that lasted for almost a full year. At the height of this period, I was convinced there was a shadow person in my room, waiting for me to go to sleep or turn my back. Choppers flew overhead, and I could feel the thrum of the blades beating in my ribs. The radios were always crackling—mostly with static—but sometimes I heard snatches of words. Sometimes they were simple commo checks, and sometimes they came from the patrol with the man whose voice cracked in the middle of, "Put the tube where?"—the radio shrieking as he half laughed and half screamed, "He's got no fucking face!" I heard my name most frequently, though, always in the voice of my sergeant. The way he drawled it out a little like there was a joke he was getting ready to share the day before a land mine killed him.

Rationally, I knew there was no shadow person lurking at the foot of my bed, that the only helicopters were the news crews reporting on early morning traffic. That there sure as hell were no radios around, and no dead men were trying to use them to talk to me. I knew it, but in the grip of my breakdown, rationality only made me feel worse about everything. My best friend's words echoed in my head. *Get over it.* They bounced around and changed, turned into a poison that did a lot of damage.

Get over it. Stop making things up. You know it's not real, so stop feeling like it is. Don't waste other people's time with this shit. Just suck it up and push on through. Eat some grass and don't bitch. Fuck, you're absolutely mental. What the hell is wrong with you?

Thoughts festered, but I pushed through them and worked hard. I threw myself into doing anything and everything I could to be considered normal. I never, ever, told anyone about what I was going through, though I started to freak out at every turn. I started thinking someone was behind me everywhere I went. I got angry at everyone, no matter who they were or what they were or were not doing. I stopped leaving my house unless I absolutely had to. Then I stopped leaving my room.

Rationality didn't help. No matter how often I told myself it wasn't real, it never helped. I eventually turned to irrational things to try and cope.

I had a small stone carving of a dragon and a smaller one of a howling wolf with an ear chipped off—little tokens from some tourist trap I didn't remember visiting when I was young. I carried them with me everywhere, in my pockets or my hand, always aware of them being with me. They became my guardians, and one touch could ease me down from my tense thoughts. How they did this was something I was very careful not to think about too much. Their protection only worked if I didn't examine my belief in them too closely. At that point in my life I needed any help I could get. Especially since I'd convinced myself I didn't need professional help.

I stopped sleeping at night because nothing bad could happen to me in the light of day, but I was vulnerable at night. My problems were like vampires and shriveled mostly away under the sunlight. Sleeping only during the day was a problem due to work and school, but it became easier when winter gave way to summer.

I used headphones and loud music to drown out the radios and choppers. My ears always rang, and sometimes the headphones slipped off when I slept. It was better, though, than hearing the dead call my name. When my ears started hurting too much, I turned to fans and white noise generators. They weren't as good at masking the words I was still hearing, but it was the only break I could get.

I slept with a knife on the table beside me at first, but that was too far away eventually. So I went to sleep holding it. I took comfort in the fact I had a weapon and could use it at any moment. At least it wasn't a gun, I rationalized. I didn't own a gun then and had no plans to get one. I was terrified of what I might do if I had access to one.

I never fell asleep with my back to the room. The bed was against the wall so I started falling asleep with my back to it, or sitting up against it on my really bad days. Even that wasn't enough, though. I thought of the space under the bed and what could hide there. Even though I crammed all I could shove under it to fill the empty space, my brain refused to calm down. So some days I would sleep on the floor. As long as I could see under my bed, I knew everything was fine.

That's how I spent my time then: my back to the opposite wall, bedroom light on, fan going, stone figures digging into my thigh, the sun coming through the curtains, and a knife in hand. I was still terrified of things I knew weren't real but saw and heard no matter how often I told myself to just get over them. I was caught in a cycle of hallucinations and irrational thoughts, but I was still aware enough to know none of it was real.

One day at a time. That's how I started to live my life.

It got better, but only after I'd almost become a hermit. Slowly, so painfully slowly, the hallucinations started disappearing first. I kept using the fans and lights though. Then the feeling that I wasn't alone started fading. I still slept with the lights on and my knife, but I started sleeping at night again. I started going outside again. Driving was still a chore, but my hands strayed to my stone figures less.

I became functional again, but I still to this day stick to some of my irrational coping mechanisms. They're habit now mostly, but they don't hurt anyone else, and I still have this vague fear that not following some of them will dump me right back into the past. So I doubt I will ever truly get over what haunts me, even with the help I managed to ask for after my second deployment.

Sometimes I still think I can feel the thrum of choppers in my ribs, but it actually feels more like the force of that IED going off. There are nights in which sleep will elude me and my ears will strain for the radio I swear I can almost hear. The old voices are replaced by a new one screaming, "I can't breathe!" I have a child's nightlight in my room and its solid white light doesn't reveal any shadows no matter how often I look for them.

I've accepted that this is the way it's going to be for me from now on. Even the professional help I sought and am still seeking may not change this. There's not much a therapist can do when I cannot talk to them about everything, and a handful of pills only helps when I can make myself take them. It's a slow process I know, but I am thankful that I am at least mostly functional.

I'm Fine
When I was little
I couldn't sleep in the Light.
I'd toss and turn complaining
the Light kept me awake.

Now I'm older and find
I can't sleep in the Dark.
Can't stand opening my eyes
and not knowing what is there.

It's not much
that separates
then from now.

A year and not much
worth mentioning happened.
Just War and all it brings—
Light and Dark weren't
what kept me up then.

(explosions all the time)
Nothing really happened.
(screams over radios)
It was only a year.
(shockwaves vibrating ribs)
I had it pretty easy really.
("He's got no fucking face!")
Nothing ever happened to me.
(dead names on paper)
I'm fine, perfectly fine.
(comforting, rapid gunfire)
I made it back alive at least.
(flag-covered boxes in a line)
I just can't sleep in the dark.

Anita Hupy Siccardi (top left) joined the U.S. Army in 1989 at age fifty. As a Captain in the Army Nurse Corps, her duty station was in Nuremberg, Germany, at the 98th General Hospital. She was a nursing supervisor in Germany and in Desert Storm. She served in active duty for three years and in the reserves for five years.

Anita H Siccardi

MY LIFE IN THE U.S. ARMY NURSE CORPS

ANITA SICCARDI

Most life altering situations take place over time . . . simultaneously with daily life, when one is going about their usual routines.
— Jeffrey A. Kottler

Why I Became an Army Nurse at Age Fifty

IN 1985 I WAS A woman in transition. Newly divorced with grown children, I was shifting my identity from wife and mother to that of a single woman. That year I moved from a small town in southern Indiana to Indianapolis and accepted a faculty position in a school of nursing. My goal while teaching was to complete both a second master's degree in primary health care nursing and a doctorate degree in higher education administration.

Two and a half years into my contract, faculty turmoil erupted in the school of nursing. A newly appointed dean made unpopular changes to the structure and function of the program. Many of my colleagues were treated with disrespect, and more than a few wanted to leave the school. However, they feared being middle-aged and unemployed or middle-aged and having to adapt to a different school culture. With courage I had gained by successfully moving to a new city on my own, I told myself, "I do not ever want to be afraid to leave a familiar place to take on a new challenge."

Coincidently, I had joined a Kiwanis organization whose members included active duty soldiers. While volunteering at the Indianapolis Handicapped Games, I mentioned to one of these members that I was feeling weary of all my duties—teaching nursing students in classes and hospital units while also creating a new congruent curriculum program for eight campuses and working on a master's and doctorate. The fellow Kiwanis member was a colonel who happened to be commander of the Army recruiting battalion for that area of the Midwest. The colonel said, "You are tired, and the Army needs nurses."

I replied "I am fifty and too old for the Army."

He said, "Maybe not."

The two of us had further conversations, and Sergeant Green, who worked with the colonel, visited me several times within the next year. My colleagues teased me, calling him my bodyguard because he was with me so often. Many times I looked over my right shoulder—and the sergeant was there.

The possibility of joining the Army was intriguing. Over the years, I had traveled extensively and had lived in six different states. The military, however, offered a culture unknown to me. The opportunity to know "worlds" I had never known sparked my interest.

After conversations with some Army nurses, I decided joining the Army would be a worthy adventure at that point in my single life. In the spring of 1989, just weeks before graduating with a second master's degree in primary care nursing, I told Sergeant Green I was close to a decision but that if I joined, I would want to be assigned to Germany in a nurse practitioner role.

The Sergeant said, "We do not send newbies overseas."

"Look at my face," I said, "and tell me I am a newbie."

"I will see if we might make an exception," he said.

I had doubts about my decision when I thought about my three children. Although they had their own lives now, I had always kept a fairly tight lariat around them, wanting to secure their safety. Was I loosening the lariat too much by going to Germany? How could I "be there" for them from thousands of miles and an ocean away?

When I told Jeffrey, my oldest son, of my decision to join the Army Nurse

Corps, he was pleased. He was a lieutenant in the Air Force and shared with me some of his military experiences and showed me the pilot's helmet he wore as a T37 flight instructor. I realized there was so much about his military life that I hadn't known. Jeffrey and I discussed guidelines for discernment in Kahlil Gibran's book *The Prophet*, including the passage, "Your children are not your children. . . . They come through you but not from you. . . . They belong not to you."

After I conversed over the phone with my son Jerry who was finishing his degree in the architectural studio at Clemson, he shouted to classmates, "My mom is going to wear combat boots!" Possibly my youngest son was relieved that I would have direction in my life. A few years earlier, he had lightheartedly said, "Mom, stop going to school, and get a real job because you are not getting any younger."

"Jerry, the youngest child has to take care of the mother," I had responded.

"Get another plan, Mom," Jerry quipped.

Now, when I expressed concern about his move to the big city of New York, my son replied, "And you are going to Germany. Which one of us should be worried?"

My daughter Julia was a teacher in northern Indiana. When I told her of my plans, she expressed concern for the distance but said, "It's okay with me as long as you're here for my wedding. I can't get married without you." Her wedding date was set for the following year, in June of 1990. We discussed plans and prearrangements so I would be able to fulfill the role of mother of the bride.

I was also concerned about my seventy-one-year-old mother who had recently been diagnosed with multiple infarct dementia. She lived in Houston with my stepfather. My brother and sister, who lived only a few miles from my mother, convinced me that they would be caregivers and that I would probably be able to visit her as frequently in the military as I could working in Indiana. My mother still recognized me at that time. When I talked to her on the phone, she'd say, "Come home so we can play."

The day I first moved to Indianapolis, I met a man who became a good friend. Jimmy and I played tennis and rode bikes together. Over the course of three years, he wanted our relationship to become closer than just friendship, but I wasn't ready for that. Although my previous marriage was behind me, I felt it had been a good marriage with three wonderful children and I just couldn't see myself moving into another close relationship. Jimmy joked about my joining the Army and did not believe that I was serious.

My transition from teacher and student to Army nurse and soldier moved rather quickly. My commissioning was planned for the day I graduated with my second master's degree. I switched my master's in education commencement hood to my master's in nursing hood and escorted family and friends into a separate room at the Convention Center to sign the oath and be sworn in by my son Jeffrey. I received a direct commission as an officer in the Army Nurse Corps based on my education and experience.

I had many questions about my immediate future, but I was excited and not anxious about the things I didn't know. For the most part, I had resolved my doubts and felt at ease with the challenge. I thought of the experience as a journey and remembered the words of an unknown author: "When God takes you to the edge of the cliff, take the leap. He will either catch you or teach you to fly."

"Come On, Mom. You Can Do It!"

AS A NEWLY COMMISSIONED OFFICER, I reported in June 1989 to Fort Sam Houston for the Basic Officer Leadership Course (BOLC). I looked forward to the transition from civilian to military life and so was disappointed when our group of new recruits—doctors, nurses, and other medical personnel—had to move into the Lexington Hotel due to a shortage of housing. Not living on the post seemed to question the reality of my being a soldier because, in all the military movies I ever saw, soldiers lived in barracks.

During my training I had no trouble mastering the content of the classes. That content consisted of learning military etiquette, protocols, and history, as well as the treatment for blast injuries and injuries due to neurological, biological, and chemical weapons. My roommate Jackie had prior service so she could provide points of reference to help me connect with new information. Jackie also showed me how to assemble equipment and appropriately prepare my uniform with insignias distinguishing rank and corps.

One afternoon a clerk came into the class to hand me a correspondence from Lieutenant Hupy, asking me to meet him that evening in his bungalow at Lackland Air Force Base. My son Jeffrey was requesting the honor of my presence. The request was addressed to Captain Hupy. I was his mother and I outranked him, yet he was requesting. How could this be? I was proud and thrilled that circumstances offered this opportunity to connect.

We often drilled with a drill instructor (DI) who shouted commands on the parade field. This was not only for discipline but to move a large number of people from point A to point B in an orderly and efficient manner. The sergeant, however, seemed to be yelling directly at me.

Shouting was not my preferred mode of communication so I found this a bit distressing. Silently, I called the sergeant "Sammy Davis, Jr." because he could have been his twin. I was in the midst of adjusting to his tactics when we had another DI step in whose commands were not sharp. They were, in fact, unclear. You can imagine the confusion as people marching in the same ranks misinterpreted his commands and moved in different directions. The next day Sammy yelled the commands, and I was proud to march with purpose and intent. Which leader would I want in conflict situations? Sammy, of course.

Certainly, the physical training was a challenge, yet I had lots of support from my fellow soldiers. These soldiers immediately identified me as "Mom," and on morning runs when I said, "Come on, guys, give me some encouragement—I'm waning," my supporters would shout, "Come on, Mom! Come on, Mom! You can do it!" When I ran my final PT test for qualifying, my fans were gathered around the track, yelling encouragement. I felt confident and wanted to show them what I could do. So I sprinted the last hundred yards—and thought I would never catch my breath again.

Life in the field at Camp Bullis proved intriguing. The tents were coed, but that did not seem awkward or offensive to me. We knew how to get undressed and redress within our sleeping bags. We were challenged to move through enemy territory, looking for a downed helicopter or a disabled ambulance. On maneuvers we crawled on our bellies with M-16 rifles and communicated through sign language. We patrolled all night and staged scenarios, like being hit with chemical weapons. We also traversed a body of water with our legs around a rope stretched from one bank to the other, pulling ourselves across, hand-over-hand. The mission to repel down a sixty-five-foot tower seemed most daunting. Not being fond of heights, I pepped myself up and prayed that I would not embarrass myself when I had to jump off the other side of the tower with only a rope in my hand.

I gained a respect for the people in uniform based on what I learned in classes and observed. They seemed to be striving to get better in every aspect of their life and really practiced the mantra of "being all you can be." I was learning about a world I did not know, and I liked what I was learning. There was never a sense that I was treated differently because I was a woman. There may have been some distinctive expectations, though, based on my age. For instance, I had fewer sit-ups and push-ups, but I never complained about that. Our class became very close, and friendships continued between those of us who were later stationed in Germany.

During my training, I obtained a basic understanding of weapons and tactics of military conflict. I learned how to live in close quarters and work as a team. I learned a lot about dedication and commitment to the mission. I was learning something about "solemn service," too. To me it meant being close to people who were not ashamed to share pride in their country or let their values show.

My friend Jimmy came to my graduation from Basic. He drove with me afterwards to Houston to visit my parents, Ray and Dollie, and my brother, Buddy, and sister, Loeta. My brother and my stepfather were excited about my entry into the military; each of them had served in the Army. In contrast, my sister, like my daughter, was apprehensive. My mother, with her dementia, was not sure what was happening, but she was happy because I was smiling with eagerness.

Jimmy traveled with me to New Orleans where I shipped my car to Germany. We said good-bye for supposedly the last time as I boarded the plane for my duty station in Nuremberg, Germany.

Duty Station 98th General Hospital Nuremberg

NUREMBERG DID NOT FEEL STRANGE to me even though the sights and sounds were new. I stayed at the German American Hotel where the atmosphere was comparable to a monastery. The patrons were quiet, and my German was so limited that I did not invite conversation. The hotel was across the street from the *bahnhof* (train station) where I could catch a train to the 98th General Hospital.

The transition to Army Nursing was easy because I was working in an American hospital and taking care of American patients. But since I had been a medical surgical nurse and adult nurse practitioner, my assignment to the newborn nursery surprised me. When I asked what prompted the assignment, Chief Nurse Colonel Knepper explained that they needed maturity in the nursery; I would be filling in for the head nurse who was going on maternity leave.

I told the chief nurse that I had maturity in years but not in experience. Then I remembered that just after nursing school, about twenty-seven years earlier, I was a charge nurse for a newborn nursery and its labor and delivery units. Colonel Knepper must have read that on my résumé.

In civilian nursing a nurse who wants to change to a specialty, such as obstetrics or pediatrics, will find that the transition will take time and training, if it happens at all. In the military, with more limited staffing needs, nurses list whatever changes they would like to make on their dream sheet and work with their supervisor to make it happen. There are lots of training opportunities in the military, not only for military skills but nursing skills as well.

During the time I served in the nursery, a couple of military practices surprised me. I reported to work one day and the sergeant told me I was to report to the rifle range. In all my years working in hospitals, that had never happened to me before!

In addition to my head nurse responsibilities, I was interim chief of education—creating education in-services and serving as a "superuser" for the new computer systems. I mentored hospital nursing and medical personnel when they had issues with the technology systems. Doctors and nurses felt extremely challenged by the recent change to an integrated computer system.

Within a few months I was appointed chief nurse for evenings and nights. This meant that I worked three twelve-hour shifts and then could take off to sightsee for four days. I might take a bike trip or drive my sports car to France, Italy, Belgium, Holland, Spain, England, or Czechoslovakia.

Sometimes my good friend Elfreide Reith accompanied me on the bike trips. I first met Elfreide when I spoke at the German Nurses Association.

She was my interpreter. Elfreide taught nursing at the Nuremberg Klinikum, a two-thousand-bed hospital in Nuremberg. Our philosophies and interests were similar, and we enjoyed riding bikes together and attending concerts and plays. At first she was reluctant to become friends with me because so many Americans she had known had returned to the United States. She did not want to lose another friend.

When I returned home to Indiana, Elfreide called every Christmas and my birthday. I was often not home at the time, but I would return her call and we talked extensively. After about four years, though, I could not reach her when I tried to return her call and my letters were returned. Elfriede had to say good-bye to another American friend.

In Berchtesgaden, Bavaria, two of my Army nurse friends met me for a long weekend. We visited some of the museums and places where Hitler lived. As we were returning to our respective posts, we saw many small Russian-made Trabant cars on the Autobahn and wondered where they were coming from. This would have been early November of 1989. We heard on the radio that The Wall had come down. East and West Germans were flowing across the border to see relatives they had not seen for many years.

When I first arrived in Germany, many soldiers were bused to the border between East and West Germany. I was astonished to observe fences of barbed wire, guard dogs, and guardhouses lined up in double and triple rows. Such a barrier between civilized countries seemed incomprehensible. Seeing all those Trabant cars meant that the fences and guardhouses, as well as the Berlin Wall, were finally coming down.

Later, when I was staying in a hotel in East Germany, I heard the distinctive singing of the famous Kelly Family and saw a long line of people with clasped hands linked across the space where the Berlin Wall had been. I ran and joined the line. We sang, "Take my hand, I am your brother. Take my hand, I am your sister." Together we sang and swayed and cried.

I was one of the officers sent to Pilsen, Czechoslovakia, for the forty-fifth anniversary of the liberation of Czechoslovakia at the end of WWII. When we arrived by bus, we saw buildings and shop windows decorated with U.S. flags, red, white and blue flowers, and posters conveying appreciation. The people of Pilsen hugged us and thanked us. President Havel and Ambassador Black gave speeches near the statues in the center of town. Dignitaries and townspeople expressed sadness that they could not show appreciation sooner. Not long after the end of WWII, they had been oppressed by the Iron Curtain. The whole situation astonished me. I was five years old at the time of the liberation, and yet here I was—receiving this tribute for my country.

Jimmy called in October of 1989 to say that he was coming to see me at Christmas. I said I could not have time off to be with him because I was saving my leave for Julie's wedding in June. He came anyway, and we took short trips around my work schedule. On one of these, we drove to Innsbruck, Austria, and caught a train to Vipiteno, Italy, traveling through the Alps and the Brenner Pass. The sights were so spectacular that we could not absorb all the beauty. We ran from one side of the train to the other, trying to see every amazing view of the snow-covered Alps.

Over the next year, problems in the Gulf escalated. In late fall of 1990, the Assistant Head Nurse informed me that the three combat units I was assigned to augment might be deployed to the Persian Gulf for Desert Shield. She asked if I really wanted to go and explained that they only needed to send seven nurses from our 98th General Hospital because the hospital was going to be kept intact as an evacuation facility for the wounded from the Gulf. Our seven 98th General Hospital nurses would augment the 128th Combat Support Hospital (CHS) out of Nelligen, Germany.

With only one year of experience as an Army Nurse, I knew there were probably things I didn't even know to consider when deciding what to do. I did believe, however, that joining the Army Nurse Corps meant that I was mentally prepared for whatever happened regarding military engagements during my time of service. I told the chief nurse that I wanted to go to the Gulf with the six other nurses.

On Sunday the 30th of December 1990, I was meditative and prayerful as I prepared for church, reviewing the readings for the Mass. My continual prayer was that my actions were not my will but God's. I did not want to thrust myself into a situation I could not handle in Desert Shield. I was afraid my age and lack of experience might hamper my completion of tasks and someone would be hurt. I was not sure of my ability to carry forty-pound duffle bags or swing a sledgehammer to set up a large tent. If lost in the desert, could I implement land navigation techniques? Could I make potable water for keeping myself and others safe?

I asked God for a sign, and within minutes the phone rang. A voice said, "Captain Hupy, be ready at the close of business tomorrow." I took that as a clear sign to continue to prepare.

When I arrived at the church for Mass that morning, I went to the back and saw a very short altar boy trying to reach his vestments. He asked, "Could you help me?" Then he asked, "Could you fasten my robe?" As I got down at his eye level to assist, he said, "I am not sure what I am supposed to do."

As I continued to look at his face, I wanted to say, "Oh, me too. I have the same concern about myself."

The altar boy said, "My brother is in the church, and he will know what to do."

I asked the priest, "Could we wait for the altar boy to get his brother?" I paused. "We all need a little help from our brother now and then."

Camp Henry, Saudi Arabia

IT'S THE WINTER OF 1990, and talks for a peaceful solution to the Gulf conflict with Iraq have not been successful. Coalition military troops are arriving in Saudi Arabia in great numbers. Our assemblage from Germany arrives at Port Dammam in Dhahran about 0530 on the 9th of January. Our assigned lodgings are warehouses filled with rows of cots. Army issue and personal articles, including two forty-pound duffle bags per person, are in disarray. I look at faces, male and female. They appear fearful.

We are told to wear our helmets outside the warehouses. With the volume of people clustered together, we are a prime target for Saddam. The next day I board a rattletrap bus with broken windows. We are fifty soldiers embarking on an eighteen-hour ride across the bumpy, frozen desert to a place called Camp Henry, farther north in Iraq. I think about the docks we left, with their stench of fish and filth, the groans of the ships being unloaded and the feel of grime under our skin. Could it get any worse than that garbage dump? I am reminded of the book *Shell Seekers* by Rosemond Pilcher. She describes luxury as "the total fulfillment of all five senses at once." At the time I could not have seen a correlation—but at the docks my senses were on overload. Now my fellow soldiers describe our cross-country ride across desolate desert as the "bus ride from hell." I cannot say this trip is hell, but I will say it is hard.

Arriving at Camp Henry, twenty-seven female nurses settle into a large tent. Our ages range from twenty-one to thirty-five with the exception of one fifty year old. The personalities and backgrounds of my tent mates are as different as our reasons for serving here. We train most days and try to sleep at night in our aberrant surroundings. We lie in sleeping bags, on cots crowded close together, warmed by a propane heater, trying to shut out Desert Thunder bombing through the night.

On January 17th we are awakened at 0337 by the clash of metal on metal— the warning for potential attacks. The smell of fright is thick as fog as we hurry in the dark and confusion to don MOPP 2 gear. We have little information other than what we hear on a portable radio—that the war has started with an Air Force allied coalition attacking Iraqi forces. The attack is described as "successful and ongoing." My tent mates show the gamut of emotions, from excitement to tears. They are concerned for fellow soldiers. Some even have husbands at the front. Broadcasts from the States bring news of loved ones fearful for our safety. From this time forward we attempt to sleep with bombing raids regaling us through the night. I give foot massages, called reflexology, to help nurses relax into sleep. Our differences begin to meld together as we share our common fears, uncertainties, and dread.

We learn a great deal about each other in a very short time. Yet we may not really know each other because of the stress and anxiety we face. We may be totally different in our real, everyday world. The theologian and philosopher Gerald Vann wrote, "A human being is a mystery which must be learned slowly, lovingly, with care and tenderness and pain, and which is never learned completely."

In early February I travel to King Khalid Military City to visit one of the 128th CSH captains who had surgery. When I enter the hospital, I go straight to the restroom and see myself in the mirror. This is after a month of spit baths and blowing dirt, conditions akin to cattle drives in the Old West. What I see is alarming. My face is dark with dirt, and my short hair is so stiff it juts straight out from my head. My uniform, which has been hand-laundered only a few times, should be thrown away. I feel so dirty. I am ashamed to be in that clean hospital. I do not know how long I stand in disbelief. My appearance is such a contrast to that of the reservists from Arkansas who supplement the caregivers in this Saudi Hospital. They live in apartments with all the amenities.

Antidote for Low Morale

BY FEBRUARY 1, 1991 THE morale among the troops was low. Everything seemed to be in slow motion as opposed to the vitality of our movements when we arrived at our duty stations at Camp Henry. There was not much attentiveness to training and not much laughter, just a great apprehension about impending combat. Sporadic shrieks of desperation broke the silence. We had been in the desert in a waiting pattern since early January. How long could we tolerate the absence of direction and purpose?

Veteran soldiers who had experienced similar circumstances elsewhere knew that a collaborative "happening" would help to raise morale. A talent show with homegrown talent seemed to be a good prescription to change the depressed mood. As the female nurses explored their possible contribution, one suggested a dance routine: "We can do a Radio City Music Hall Rockettes-like performance." Another person said, "We can be a girls' chorus with military songs like the Andrews Sisters."

After further discussion and assessment of our talents, we decided a style show might be in order. With a limited supply of attire, there would be just two ensembles. The nurses chose desert latrinewear and beach playwear. The latrinewear consisted of a satin robe, a neck ring for toilet paper, combat boots, and a helmet with a light. I offered to model the beach playwear. "I have a grandma bathing suit," I said. "I will do it."

We decorated the large mess tent with anything we could find that looked festive, and we created a stage. There would be singing groups, dance groups, and comic routines.

My outfit was a gray-green, Army-issue gas mask with black trim, a black bathing suit with a blue and magenta stripe, and a pair of black combat boots to match the suit. I also carried a gray-green, Army-issue towel over my right arm. I was not prepared for the audience's response.

I had imagined walking across the stage, getting a lot of laughs, and walking off. But when I walked on the stage, the crowd went wild. I had to keep sashaying and pausing on the stage until they settled down. The audience shouted, "All Clear! All Clear!" This phrase is used when the danger of a gas attack is over, and soldiers can take off their gas masks. The commentator could not be heard over the roar. After he finally finished describing my ensemble, I walked off the stage without removing my mask. The model of the bizarre beach playwear remained a mystery.

The atmosphere around camp was much better the day after the talent show. People laughed and imitated the musical routines, with no symptoms of the dismal mood of previous weeks.

The Incident

IT HAPPENED ABOUT MID-DAY AND a few weeks before the ground war started. A colonel came to my tent and called me outside. When I stepped out, he began yelling at me—something about him not getting his Jeep.

I said, "I am going back into my tent now. When you are ready to talk, I will come back out."

In a few minutes I heard the Colonel say in a soft voice, "Captain." As I stepped out of my tent, he said, "You took my Jeep and driver."

"I am not sure how I could have taken your Jeep," I replied.

"I had a Jeep and driver to take my psychologists to the compound to meet with other psychologists this afternoon at 1400 hours, and you took my Jeep."

I said, "I suggest you talk to Top. He is the one who assigns vehicles and drivers." I wished him well and walked back into my tent.

Prior to attaining my request for transportation, I had gone to "Top," the First Sergeant in charge of motor pool, and asked for a Jeep and driver to take some of the nurses to have their eyes examined. They had been deployed without being examined for eyewear (inserts) to correct vision when wearing gas masks.

When Top refused my request, I struck his desk with my fist and said, "You may not care if my nurses can see to take care of the wounded, but I do!" As I pounded the desk, a lens fell out of my Army-issue glasses.

Top reversed his decision and said to be at the motor pool at 1400 hours.

I inquired about the rude colonel. I was informed that he was a reservist and psychiatrist. He had been vacationing off the coast of Spain on his yacht when he was called for active duty in Desert Storm. Was his incivility due to being called away from his vacation? Stoked by my gender? Exacerbated by the foreboding ground war?

Medcen West, Saudi Arabia

February 14, 1991 (about eleven days before the ground war starts during Desert Storm)

AT ABOUT 10 P.M., I am one of twelve soldiers moving west in the desert just south of the Iraq border. We are not sure of our location so we prepare to camp for the night. We circle the three trucks and set up cots with sleeping bags. We are assigned times to be roving guards with a partner and our M-16 rifles.

I am roused about 2 a.m. when someone shaking me says, "Captain Hupy."

My first instinct is to respond with, "I don't know where she is." It is freezing cold. But being the good soldier, I put on my boots and flack vest and field jacket. I check my M-16 and report for duty. A lieutenant and I circle around the encampment "at the ready" for two hours.

The sky is lit with explosives. The thunderous bombing is nonstop and in the future will give me pause with Fourth of July fireworks. We see convoys on the move toward Iraq. The massive movement of tanks continues through the night. Such a small amount of light in the vast dark desert creates a distortion making me believe that the convoys are coming in my direction.

I am jolted by the realization that if persons approach me, I will offer the challenge word and if they do not respond with the password, I will shoot them. I will raise my M-16 rifle and shoot them? This mild-mannered person, me, this nurse who teaches about kindness and caring is going to shoot with intent to kill or at least do harm? I am not really frightened during these several hours but my senses are certainly on high alert.

When I left my friends at Indiana School of Nursing, I said, "I want to see worlds I've never known and things that I cannot even imagine." This rendezvous is one of those rare and singular experiences that I could not have imagined.

February 24, 1991

I AWAKE AT 0400. THE bombing seems to be nonstop. At 0100 Greenwich Mean Time, which is 0300-0400 in Saudi, I turn on the radio and hear that the ground war has begun. I lie in the darkness, crying. The devastation and loss of lives has begun. There is no stopping it.

President Bush gives an address, and fresh tears stream down my cheeks. He says, "Pray for those who have put their lives at risk for freedom." In his briefing, Secretary of Defense Dick Cheney says, "The ground war has begun, and it is massive." He gives no details in order to protect the troops. According to Radio Baghdad, Saddam is telling his people to "fight violently as martyrs for this is a war we can win."

128th Combat Support Hospital

ON FEBRUARY 25, THE 128TH was ready. Our equipment was certainly modern, and our hospital had operating rooms, ventilators, labs, pharmacy, sterilization departments, and x-ray machines. We even had air conditioning. Soon, however, we were introduced to the devastation of war as many casualties began to arrive. I can best compare the scene to the movie MASH—to the beating of rotor blades as helicopters bring incoming wounded. The soldiers' wounds were mostly from landmines with shrapnel in hands, feet, legs, and faces. We received two soldiers who were critical. One was a Brit who was coded for twenty minutes without success. The other soldier was dead on arrival (DOA) with a massive head wound. He was from Kansas. I prayed for his soul as I taught my staff how to prepare the body for the morgue. These nurses were new graduates from Licensed Practical Nursing schools, and we had prepared for the casualties with difficult discussions about death and dying. A hundred hours after the ground assault began, Coalition forces drove the Iraqi army from Kuwait and called a ceasefire.

On March 4th the sky took on, what some called, an "end of the world appearance." That supposition had arisen because of the devastation and where we were located, near the Tigress and Euphrates rivers—where creation began. The stormy sky turned bright orange and then pitch black. Many reported they saw turbulence in the shape of cyclones. The rain came in sheets, and the wind leveled some of our tents. We had to dig trenches to redirect the water and save the rest of the tents. We had a foot of water in the Deployable Medical Systems for the Combat Support Hospitals (DEPMEDs)—in other words, our hospital.

On March 16th we received hundreds of letters and packages. Earlier, while the five-ton trucks were in use for supplies and troops, the mail had to wait. I received letters from friends and family, including twenty cards from Jimmy. As evidence of the support from back home, we received packages from organizations all over the U.S. For instance, I opened twenty-five letters from Girl Scouts and several packages of toiletries from a girls' choir in San Diego and a spa in Pittsburgh. My little corner of the tent looked like a mailroom.

Colonel Gifford reported that we might be going home in six to eight weeks. I spent the days reading, writing about the 128th Combat Support Hospital's wartime operation, giving lectures, and assisting with sports tournaments and any other activities that helped to sustain sanity while we waited to be deployed back to Germany. I engaged in many good-byes and we-will-stay-in-touch conversations with the friends I had made. Sadness was mixed with elation at the thought of returning home.

April 22, 1991, we left Saudi Arabia. I appreciated the clean plane. I cried as I studied the beautiful green trees, the grass, and the landscape of Rome. I stood at the doorway of the cargo area taking in the signs of spring. It had been four months since I had seen green vegetation. I contemplated my unbelievable experiences. I do not think any of us comprehended the level of anxiety we experienced until the surroundings gave us peace.

On the plane we watched videos showing the support of people back in the States. We actually knew little about the war situation compared to the folks back home who had CNN. When we landed in Stuttgart, you could not hear the landing gear coming down or the cutting back on the engines because screams of jubilation were so great. We stepped onto a red carpet where Major General Payne greeted us. We could hear the German band playing as we boarded the double-decker luxury bus for the last leg of our journey. The bus was a great contrast to the five-ton trucks that transported us across the rutted desert. We were excited that we would be back in Nuremberg soon.

Returning to Nuremberg

THE SEVEN NURSES, REFERRED TO as the "Saudi Seven," who had been deployed to augment the 128th Combat Support Hospital in Desert Storm, returned to the 98th General Hospital in Nuremberg at 0400 on the 23rd of April. All the hospital staff had been waiting for hours to greet us.

Our friends who had been supporting us with cards, letters, and gifts cried with us as we reunited. We were tired from a long flight and bus ride and four months in an extremely austere environment. I recalled those earlier words that had inspired me—the desire to enter "worlds I had never known and things I could not even imagine." How could I explain to my friends what I had experienced? It was so different from the conditions of our daily, civilized lives.

After much celebration, I was escorted to my attic apartment in Zirndorf. There were flowers and ribbons and cards of welcome there—and more mail—a box of it forwarded from Saudi Arabia. I sat on the sofa and tried to take in my surroundings. It seemed I had been away for a long, long time in an alien world. I relished my return.

I filled the bathtub with warm water, and even the water flowing into the tub was amazing. I was in the tub for hours, getting in touch with the simple luxury of so much clean water after four months of spit-baths and cold showers. I took my address book with me to call friends and family, to let them know I was back in Germany. I told Jimmy that I was coming home from the Army in a year to marry him.

My neighbors who had said goodbye a few months before greeted me warmly, even those who could not speak English. The elderly lady who lived in the apartment on the floor below mine had tried to talk to me before I left. I had to say, *"Nix verstandin,"* "I do not understand." She had squeezed my arm, saying,

"*Leider nein, leider nein,*" expressing her regret that I could not understand what she wished to convey. Now she hugged me in that common language of gladness. Her embrace told me she was happy I was back home and safe. My older German neighbors who had experienced World War II certainly knew all about the devastation of war.

Upon my return I wanted to know more about what my friend Elfreide had experienced in World War II. I asked her what it was like. Her most vivid memories were the air raids and spending so much time in the tunnels under the city. I wanted to know if she had encountered the "brickies." These were the women and children who cleaned the mortar off the bricks so they could be used to rebuild the city. Elfreide said, "Anita, I was a brickie. I cleaned the bricks and received a *pfennig* a brick." She was about five years old at the time.

It was a challenge to keep a clean apartment when I got home to Germany. I had gotten out of the habit of making the bed and preparing clean linens. The sleeping bag had been easy—I just rolled it up and everything was tidy. Cooking and cleaning the kitchen took some adjustment. The dishes had to be washed and put away. In the desert, my meals (MREs) came ready to eat, with wrappings that went in the trash.

I rejoined my social clubs and was appointed President of the 98th General Hospital Auxiliary. I planned on returning right back to work, but the chief nurse said to just take some time off, time to let my previous life catch up with me. I traveled to Amsterdam and saw the Keukenhof Gardens and Tulip Fields—acres and acres of flowers. This lush beauty was in such contrast to the desolate desert. I wanted to take in and capture all the color. While on the bus, many people wanted to engage me in conversation. I just wanted to be quiet and reflect on my experiences. To some extent I felt I was still an Army nurse in a CSH, receiving wounded from the combat zones.

My work responsibilities were the same, serving as hospital supervisor during evenings and nights. I was appointed as an officer to the Joint Commission for Accreditation of Hospitals Organization (JCAHO) and asked to conduct assessments and improvements in preparation for an evaluation visit. I also created a manual for patient education and put this online for easy access by the nurses. These were good responsibilities for me. I had a great deal of flexibility in my schedule as I worked on various projects.

During my last year in the Army, I spent time with friends and tried to see all the things in Europe I had earlier missed. Many friends from the U.S. came to visit, and we took trips together. I was so excited when I could share my favorite sites with my daughter and her new husband. They came during my last Christmas holiday overseas. Few countries celebrate the season with as much fervor as Germany does. We visited the world-famous Nuremberg *Chriskindlemardt,* one of the largest Christmas markets in Germany. Sharing German culture and folklore with my daughter helped me to re-experience that excitement of discovery I felt when I first arrived in Germany.

In the late summer of 1991, I took "leave" to see the house my fiancé had selected for us in Carmel, Indiana. I had instructed Jimmy to buy a lot with trees. I did not care what the house looked like. I just wanted trees and green grass—lots of it. The sensory deprivation I felt in the Saudi desert was already having an impact on decisions affecting my future.

Back Home in Indiana

OUT-PROCESSING FROM THE 98TH GENERAL Hospital duty station in Nuremberg was long and disorganized. There was a lot to coordinate—the turning in of equipment, the release from duties, and the move from my apartment. While the hospital staff had been excellent to work with for the past three years, I felt some concern about the people responsible for the logistics of where I needed to be as I separated from the Army. It took a few months for the Army to complete all the plans for moving me back to the States. Of course, the Army faced moving several thousand military personnel from Germany in the spring of 1992. My orders said that I would land in Philadelphia, pick up my car in Bayonne, New Jersey, and then drive to Fort Dix, New Jersey, to be discharged from the Army as an active duty soldier.

When I finally reached Indianapolis, the money from my German bank had not yet arrived, and I had no civilian ID—no U.S. driver's license and no check-cashing card. I had no credit because of credit card fraud on my closed account. For all intents and purposes, I had no identity. To make things worse, the grocery stores were overwhelming with their huge inventory of products. I

faced ten times the choices I had in Germany. To reach a person within any organization or business, I had to sift through layers of telephone numbers. Technology had tripled in complexity. America was so confusing that I seriously
wanted to return to my simple life in Germany, where stores closed at noon on
Saturday and did not open until Monday morning and a favorite pastime for
people was walking in the woods. Fortunately, the recent time I spent in worlds
unfamiliar to me also solidified my resolve not to be afraid of challenges.

When I came back, I felt it was important to take time to reflect on my
Army experiences, including the people I had grown to know so well and the
culture of the military. An important reason I enlisted was to experience a new
world. I reflected that my three years of service had strengthened my sense of
caring for others. Dedication and commitment to the cause had meant looking
out for those I lived and worked with—doing what I could for them, even at
great personal inconvenience.

While I was away, my three children had thrived as they adjusted to new
careers or marriage. My brother and sister seemed much the same, but my
mother's dementia was worse and she lived for only another year.

Jimmy was waiting. We were married in the woods at Fort Harrison State
Park, by Fall Creek. Now we live in a house surrounded by lots of trees and
flowers.

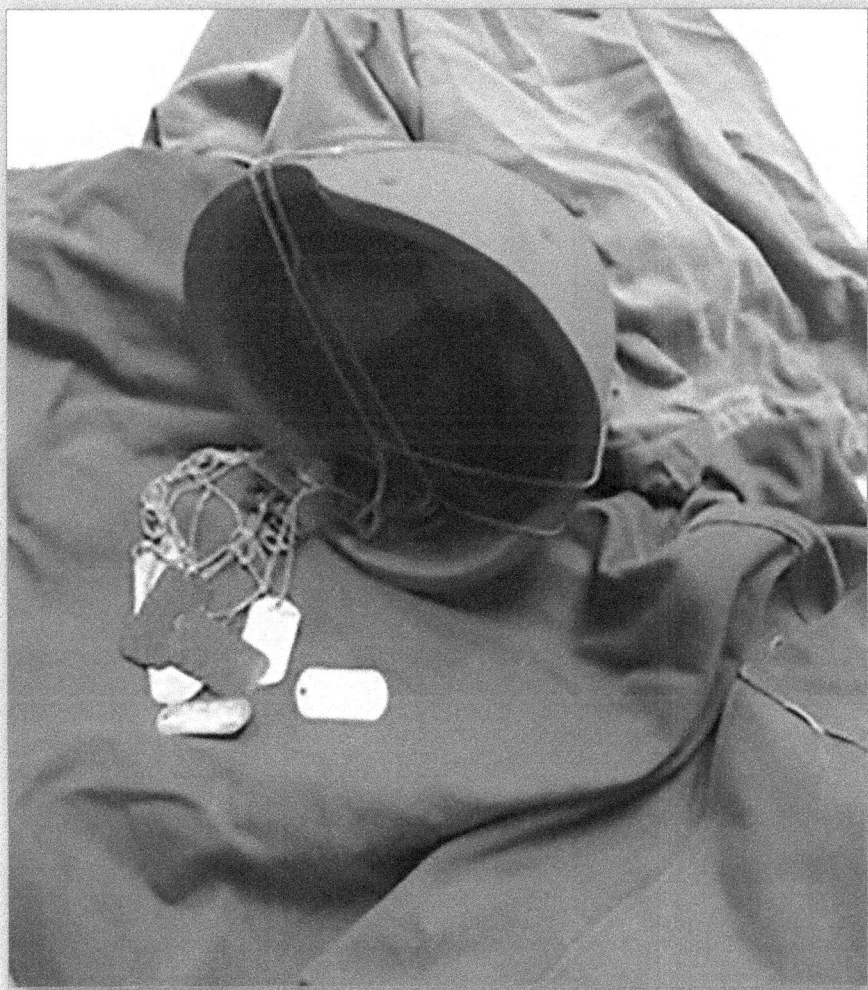

Elizabeth Von Tobel Smith, PFC, enlisted in the Marine Corps Women's Reserve in February of 1944 at twenty-one years old. She attended Boot Camp and Quarter Master School at Camp Lejeune. At Lakehurst Naval Air Station she was a Quarter Master OFC, a bookkeeper. She completed her service in January of 1946 in Washington, D.C., at Commandant Headquarters.

KEEPING UP WITH MY BROTHERS: MEMORIES OF A WWII MARINE

ELIZABETH SMITH

A Day to Remember

THE SWITCHBOARD LIGHTS UP LIKE a Christmas tree. What's going on?

I am a switchboard operator in the telephone office in Peoria, Illinois. This is my once-a-month slow, dull Sunday. We have never had this many incoming calls on a Sunday before. I frantically start answering them as do the other ten operators down the line.

"What's going on?" everyone asks. "Is this another show?" They're referring to Orson Wells' radio play *War of the Worlds,* a drama with aliens attacking Earth. Three years earlier, half the population of the United States mistakenly thought the broadcast was real.

By this time a supervisor, coming down the line, whispers in each operator's ear, "The Japanese have attacked Pearl Harbor." A place I had never heard of is about to change not only my life but also the lives of millions of Americans.

That Sunday was December 7, 1941. It seemed like overnight every able-bodied man signed-up or was drafted, including my three brothers. John, the youngest, had been drafted into the Army in October of 1941 and was fighting with the 41st Infantry in the Philippines. Paul was drafted into the Army right after Pearl Harbor and was a topographer in Australia with Army engineers, drawing maps of the islands. Francis, the oldest, enlisted in the Marine Corps in 1942 and was stationed on board the *USS West Virginia* in the Pacific.

I wrote daily to all three of my brothers on the one page V Mail used by the U.S. Post Office for the military. When the page was full, I mailed each one and started a new letter. Our lives became obsessed with getting the latest war news. Any time we heard a newsboy outside shouting, "Extra! Extra!" we would run for a copy. We went to movies to see the latest war news on *Movietone News.* My parents displayed a 12"x12" cloth plaque with three stars in the front window. This was changed to four when I enlisted.

Love and Family Hardships

UNDERSTANDING THE CIRCUMSTANCES UNDER WHICH I joined the Marines takes a little background. I was born in 1922 into a very ordinary family. My brothers were four, five, and six years old at the time. Our hard-working mother and father saw to it that we had enough. My father sold automobiles, so my parents drove a nice vehicle and were in the process of buying our home. The stock market's final crash in 1929 was like a row of dominoes falling. One by one, week after week, each facet of our lives fell toward the hole of "The Great Depression." Millions were out of work, including my dad. We lost our home and moved into a rental house.

Through relatives, my mom was lucky enough to get a job as a waitress at the YWCA, a place for single young ladies living away from their parents. Mom's job paid the rent and house expenses. A surprise bonus was that her boss let her take home the leftover food they couldn't use the next day. Many nights we would get our supper around 8:30. Still, we were four lucky kids whose parents showered us with what didn't cost a cent: love. If there was an extra quarter, Dad would walk to the store for ice cream. We had no car at this time.

In about 1933 I noticed some changes. I had three school dresses instead of two, and the soles of my shoes didn't need cardboard to cover the holes. Dad had gotten a job, and Mom no longer worked outside the home. My two oldest brothers dropped out of school to work as movie ushers to help out with bills.

Finally, life was looking up, though many were still homeless and unemployed and there were still bread lines. Americans were just starting to breathe a little happiness when Pearl Harbor was attacked and war declared.

From coast to coast, the nation would learn to pull together as one team. Women took men's jobs. Things that had previously been discarded were recycled: used cooking grease, anything rubber, old leather. Rationing allowed two pairs of shoes a year. Meat, flour, sugar, canned and fresh fruit and vegetables, all were rationed. Yards were dug up and Victory Gardens planted. The military came first.

Joining Up

NOT UNTIL THE MARINE CORPS announced it was accepting women did I decide I wanted to join up. Since childhood, I had always thought anything my brothers could do, I could do, too. If they were trying to see who could climb highest in our apple tree, I was up there, too. I explored the vacant lot and dug caves right along with them. When my brothers yelled that they were going to the school playground, I said, "I'm going, too."

With three sons already on the fighting front in the Pacific, my parents did not receive the news that I wanted to join the military happily. It took over a year before my mother understood how much I wanted to serve and she and Dad gave permission. In December of 1943, I decided I wanted to do what my brothers were doing. I waited until after Christmas and signed up for the Marines. That year the *Peoria Star* carried an article entitled, "Local Family Has Four in Uniform."

The Marine Corps was the last (and most reluctant) branch of the military to admit women. The story goes that the Marine commandant made a public statement: "There will be no women in the Marine Corps." The next day President Roosevelt called him to the oval office. Looking the commandant directly in the eye, he said, "There will be women in the Marine Corps." End of conversation.

The idea of the Marine Corps Women's Reserve (MCWR) was that it could free up men for combat. Women would be trained in noncombatant positions.

However, there were a million excuses that delayed the process of implementing the change. The first recruits were stationed at Hunter College in New York. As the wheels slowly turned, camps were added in San Diego, California, and near Jacksonville, North Carolina.

Boot Camp

FINALLY, IN FEBRUARY 1944, I was on a train taking me to the Marine Corps base at Camp Lejeune in North Carolina. During the entire trip, I kept asking myself if this was the right thing to be doing. Over the next six weeks, I lost count how many times I would answer that question with a resounding "No."

From the station we traveled to camp by bus, each woman carrying an overnight case with personal garments and "old lady" shoes. We were assigned a bed in our barracks, told who our sergeant was, fed, and put to bed.

It was 5:00 or 5:30 a.m. when the thousand watt light shone on my face and a voice screeched over the loudspeaker, "HIT THE DECK!" All ninety of us leaped from our bunks and started the day at a run.

It was high gear for six weeks. Move fast. Make beds tight—no wrinkles. Scrub the floor. Pass the mop to the next trainee. Off to the showers. Take turns cleaning the head and shower room. Get dressed. Stand at attention for inspection at 6:30 a.m. then march in formation to the mess hall. Marching, marching. Day after day seemed to roll into one long, long day.

The "Hit the Deck" voice was our sergeant, whom we privately called "Bossy Boss." She stood about 5'2", but if you closed your eyes, you would swear she was six feet tall. She must have had eyes in the back of her head, and she could hear a pin drop. She corralled us to where we needed to be for classes: History of the Marines and What Makes a Marine "Special." She drilled us two hours a day, that is if we "got it." If not, we drilled an extra hour.

Three days a week we had a male drill sergeant who drilled us fiercely for two hours followed by lectures on proper Marine conduct. Along with the usual verbal drill, we had to memorize a silent drill routine. All the platoon's movements were executed in a kind of silent martial choreography.

At the end of five weeks, the platoons were judged, with the winning platoon awarded a special banner to carry at all times. Being the tallest, I was platoon leader, and when we placed first, you'd have thought we each had won a million dollars. We were filled with pride.

The sixth week flew by for everyone as our platoon started winding down. That last Saturday all women on base had to be in formation for inspection by the top brass. Finally, the anxiety of graduation day ended, and we were dismissed to return to barracks for orders. Mine read: *Quarter Master School, Camp Lejeune, three months duty.*

It was in boot camp that I learned an important lesson I use every day, even now at age ninety-four: I truly can do anything I put my mind to.

Quarter Master School

I STARTED SCHOOL IN THE middle of March. The next three months were very regimented, not unlike boot camp. There were twenty-four women Marines in our class, and we were housed together in a smaller barracks.

We were mostly on our own as we got ready in the morning—as we made our bunk, got the area squared away, went for breakfast, and then, at 7:25, fell into formation. We marched at 7:30 a.m. and 4:30 p.m., five days a week for three months. We did have freedom from 5-10 p.m., Monday through Thursday. On weekends we could occasionally leave base with a pass.

With our evening and weekend free time, we had choices. We could take in a movie on base, read a book, or write letters. A group of us might go outside for walks, stopping at the Slop Shute for a coke, beer, ice cream, or other snack. Five or six of us had become good friends and hung out together. Male Marines were allowed in our Slop Shute so some nights our group and a few men would sit around a large table and shoot the breeze for an hour or so.

Our classroom was in the men's area and at least a mile from our barracks, a distance we marched twice each day. The big surprise was what greeted us in the classroom. Did I say "greet"? "Grunt" was more like it. Our master sergeant, close to sixty, was over six feet tall. He had a large build and a physique that suggested he had enjoyed consuming a certain amber liquid for many years. He had hash marks from wrist to elbow and was gruff but easy to under-stand. "Take any desk, Privates," he said as he lit up a big cigar.

I learned to keep a strict record of every item the Marine Corps used or had on hand. It was a different way of bookkeeping, with new terminology. Previously, I had been promoted to a service representative for the Peoria Phone Company, so dealing with large accounts was nothing new to me. Bookkeeping class was well taught, and we studied hard. Sitting here writing seventy years later, I can't say just how or when the class made a surprising transformation into a more relaxed group. One woman in our class, Angie, was a born comedian who got off one-liners just loud enough to be heard by everyone. It wasn't long before our sergeant was smiling with the rest of us.

I don't remember how we found out the sergeant's birthday was coming up, but we talked our mess hall baker into baking a couple of cupcakes. He even provided a little candle. Some of us chipped in, and we bought the biggest cigar the commissary had. On morning break we put the gifts on his desk—with no note, no names. That night the master sergeant came to the Slop Shute and had a couple of beers with us.

On the last day of class there were no lessons. If you didn't have it by then, you weren't ever going to have it. Dismissal was early, and we were told we would get our orders. I do know when the master sergeant said goodbye to us it was with respect, something that had been missing in the early days of class.

We marched back to our barracks that Friday with bittersweet thoughts. We were sorry to say goodbye to the friends we had made and the good times we enjoyed, but anxious to get our orders. Our goodbyes to our classmates came Sunday night. We were all leaving for different locations on Monday. My orders that Friday read:

Report to Lakehurst Naval Air Station
Lakehurst, New Jersey
Quarter Master Office

Lakehurst Naval Air Station

UPON ARRIVAL AT LAKEHURST, I found the barracks completely different from the barracks in North Carolina. You entered a lobby area with different wings off the lobby. The Marine Corps women were housed in their own wing. Our wing to the right had separate rooms, two women to a room. It was great not to be in a large squad room with fifty or ninety women. My "Bunkie" was a woman who worked in the first sergeant's office. Anita and I became fast friends and kept in touch over the years. She was 5'1"; I was 5'7". They called us Mutt and Jeff.

My first morning reporting for duty in the Quarter Master Office did not go well. As I opened the door, two male Marines looked up from their desks. One was a staff sergeant, the other a sergeant. I handed my papers to the staff sergeant, gave him my name, and told him I was reporting for duty in the quarter master's office. All seemed okay. We exchanged names, and I was assigned my desk. About ten feet from our desks was the captain's desk. No sign of him. After about ten minutes of casual conversation, the staff sergeant said to me, "If you smoke, it's okay to smoke in the office." So I lit up. BIG MISTAKE.

As you have probably already guessed, it was NO SMOKING. The captain walked in a few minutes later and never even looked at me. As he walked by, he said, "Put that cigarette out," in a very angry voice. And, of course, there was no ashtray.

I stayed standing at attention at my desk and said, "PFC Von Tobel reporting from Quarter Master School."

He replied, "Captain Greenberg. At ease, sit down." That was the only dirty trick anyone played on me in my military career.

The captain was an older retired master sergeant whose entire life had been spent as a Marine, and now he had been called back to active duty as a temporary captain because of the war. He evidently knew the cigarette incident was instigated against me by the staff sergeant because I was "one of those women" invading his territory. There was never another word said about the incident.

About two months later the sergeant was transferred, about the same time Edith, another woman Marine, arrived as the captain's secretary. The four of us worked exceptionally well together for over a year.

Now, seventy years later, I can only look back on that time with great pleasure. It was a strict, well-run office, with an eight-to-five, five-day workweek. My duties were numerous, but the top priority was bookkeeping. As this was a Navy base, the Marines were there for guard duty and to manage our Quarter Master

Office. We provided and kept track of every item needed by the Marines. All were in one hardcover book, oblong-shaped, about twelve inches long by four inches across, and as good as three to four inches thick. The pages flipped up like a writing tablet with columns. The captain was very, very particular. Vertically, all numbers had to be straight under the one above. Horizontally, they had to be in the middle of their spaces, not touching the number on either side, and each number had to look like it came from type. All lines for a column had to be drawn the same length and with a ruler. (Reader, are you still awake?)

There were no calculators or computers. It was all brainpower and hand-done. I had to balance off this book for the year and send it to Quarter Master Headquarters in Washington, D.C. The captain's office was graded. Our official grade came back "Exceptional." I had made one mistake. At the end of one column, I put "11" and it should have been "10". The captain was very happy. We then received a new book with current inventory to start the new year. The strict bookkeeping concepts I learned in Quarter Master School served me well. In fact, I still do figures that way.

The Marines' clothing was in our storeroom. Twice a month Marines would bring in their not-so-gently-used clothing to be replaced by us.

The colonel of the detachment decided I was to be his chauffeur. I drove him to his appointments in his official car—a large station wagon. I also had to learn to drive a double-clutch pickup truck in order to pick up items at the Philadelphia Naval Yard.

About June 1945, Captain Greenberg was relieved of his active duty and sent back to retirement. A young captain was assigned to the office.

On a very warm August evening, four of us Marine women decided to go into the small town outside our base to see the seven o'clock movie. About 7:15 the movie stopped and the houselights came on. The manager walked onstage and made an announcement: "The war is over! The Japanese have surrendered!" That was August 15, 1945.

The War Is Over

WITH THAT GREAT STATEMENT, "THE war is over," ringing in our ears, everyone scrambled out of the building as fast as possible. This was a small town, but everyone was in the street—yelling, blowing whistles, cruising up and down in cars, honking horns. Bedlam. The four of us headed back to the base where we were told we had forty-eight hours liberty. We just looked at one another and said almost simultaneously, "Let's go to Times Square." We were only two hours by bus from there. That past year we had spent two, sometimes three, weekends a month in New York.

We left the base at about 8:30 p.m. and arrived at a jam-packed Times Square about 7:00 a.m. It had taken eleven hours to travel what would normally take two. Roads were clogged; no buses or trains were on schedule, and if they did come by, they were so packed no one else could get on. I have never been any place since that had the excitement, the vibes, and the constant chatter of happiness in the air. I did not witness that famous couple—the sailor kissing the nurse—but about all of us received kisses or hugs from strangers. We got back to the base almost thirty hours later, without ever seeing a bed.

In a few short weeks, the women serving in the Marine offices on the base were transferred to Marine barracks in Washington, D.C. About November 1st, I was transferred again, this time to the Commandant's Headquarters, Quartermaster Office, in D.C. My duty time there was short, only three months, but it was great. The Marine Corps Band was quartered at the same location. Picture, if you will, a large, grass-covered marching field with offices down both long sides, with the commandant's beautiful private home at the top end. The band played and marched about half a day most days of the week. With the war over, outdoor lights shone at night. The beautiful, bright-lit monuments of our capital were such a memorable sight—especially with the first snowfall.

By the third week of January 1946, I was on a train heading home. There were no doubts in my mind on this trip, as there'd been two years before as I headed to the Marine Corps. My three brothers were already home, and I couldn't get the train to go fast enough. My brother John with the Army 41st Infantry, who'd been fighting the Japanese in the South Pacific islands for almost four years, arrived first. By December 1, Paul and Francis had returned. What a month December was for Mom and Dad! We were so blessed. None of my brothers had a scratch. All were walking and standing tall.

On the day I arrived home, my mother decreed that dinner that night would be for the six of us only. No relatives, no friends. That overladen table held some of the favorite dishes of all four of us siblings. Mom, who was the greatest cook ever, outdid herself with pan-fried chicken, mashed and candied sweet pota- toes, freshly canned asparagus, coleslaw with special sweet-cream dressing. The crown jewel of the meal was my favorite dessert: Mom's homemade angel food cake with seven-minute whipped green frosting.

As we sat around the old dining room table that night, there wasn't a dry eye. We joined hands, and Mom, with tears glistening on her cheeks and a big smile, said, "We are so blessed after these terrible years to be here together, healthy and happy, as a family again." And each one of us returning children, with joy and thanks in our hearts, knew how true her words were. From that dinner, we picked up our ordinary lives. The war was over after four long years.

An Unexpected Chapter

THE HOURS I'VE SPENT WITH the amazing young ladies in this workshop have been eye opening and have brought an unexpected chapter to my life at age ninety-four. The women currently in the military are to be saluted. Some carry guns and heavy backpacks, work side by side with men in dangerous places like Iraq and Afghanistan. Seventy-two years ago our aim was to replace a man in an office so he could go fight. For good or bad, we opened a door.

Cindy "Loc" Hornung (center) enlisted in the Army Reserves in 1994 at thirty years old. She trained for active duty at Ft. Sam Houston, San Antonio, Texas, from February 1995-August 1996 and graduated from the Practical Nurse program. She began service as an Indiana Community Health Worker/ Certified Recovery Specialist in 2015 and as a Certified VA Peer Specialist in the (MST) Military Sexual Trauma Program in 2016.

IF I CAN DO IT

CINDY "LOC" HORNUNG

Chameleon

I RELOCATE TO SAN ANTONIO when a college friend says something like, "Hey, want to move to Texas?" She lives there because her husband enlisted in the Air Force.

I say something like, "Okay," because I can't think of a reason not to go. I can never think of a reason not to go. Notice I said, "A reason." No person, place or thing ever gets a good enough grip on me to make me stay. At some point I become prideful about this fact. My Grandmother Juanita always said, "Pride cometh before a fall," and she was never so right. I fall another twenty years while holding onto that attitude. But we get to that later. Besides, *going* always looks like more fun. So, what the hell, I leave Indianapolis.

#

In San Antonio, Army and Air Force trainees are as commonplace as blue-bells, piñatas, and sunburnt tourists. Locals embrace them all. They familiarize themselves with the training intervals at Fort Sam Houston (FSH) and Lack-land Air Force Base (LAFB). Some families volunteer to provide holiday meals and housing for trainees unable to travel home. Military recruiting classes that pass training phases earn weekend passes. The troops spread out into the city to whoop it up at country western bars, attend sporting events, carouse on the River Walk, get initiated into fiesta festivities, visit the Alamo, and just hang out at the Rivercenter Mall. Though a Yankee by birth, I adapt to the "Military City, USA" mindset. Every job, social event, and personal errand brings me into contact with the military in some form or fashion.

#

A couple of years and a dozen or so jobs later find me drinking at country western bars three or four times a week. Drinking alone bores me. But I'm not here for the nightlife, loud music, press of the crowd, and competing colognes. I like to two-step. I never saw people dance like that before, except maybe on *Lawrence Welk*. With a little more liquid courage, I shuffle and spin on the cornmeal-dusted floorboards.

One night a group of young women catches my attention. They drink, dance, and laugh with an intense abandon. It pulls at the middle of my chest like *want*—covetous, grieving, greedy, starved, and familial, too long-neglected *want*. Who are they? I must find out how they got this camaraderie. I join them to play darts and toss back longnecks. I notice an accent from some place way north. *Explains why they can't two-step.*

I observe them name call, tease, belittle each other, and burst out in laughter. Then they tell stories of their recent experiences. Now I see it. Their connection is born of shared experiences, of painful, miserable, fear-filled moments. Turns out they relocated via the Army from Minnesota and Wisconsin. They train at Fort Sam Houston (FSH) in the Practical Nursing Program. All that shared pent-up energy, *fervor* even, starts to make sense. Ten weeks of Basic Combat Training (BCT), plus the first phase of Combat Medic School (CMS), helped these women develop a kinship bond. No weakness. No shame. They see it all in each other. They bear it all together. Now tonight, they let it go!

#

Over succeeding days, thoughts worm their way through my mind. *This thing should belong to me already. It should've been mine a long time ago.* My kinship bond exists in blood with my brothers. *Why doesn't it exist in spirit?* Didn't we, my brothers and me, fight bullies and drunks? Didn't we experience the bitter bile from hunger, the mockery from kids in town, the erratic whims of our mother and absentee fathers? Didn't we fear for our very lives?

During the lulls between battles, we entertained ourselves. My brothers and I played cowboys and Indians. We built forts in the woods. Shot BB guns. Played with green plastic Army men. Made roads in dirt mounds for Tonka trucks. Snuck cigarettes and played with fire. Yet each of us experienced isolation, a profound loneliness. The wounded unconscious adults around us acted like selfish children. They swore, fought, put adult sexual values onto us kids, and created such torrents of chaotic circumstances that it became, "Every child for themself. Get out if you can."

I developed the mindset of a warrior. I tried to keep my fellows in a tight unit. I tried to keep us focused on the objective, to survive. I tried to follow the orders of command: "Be a good girl. Kids are to be seen and not heard. Do unto others. . . ." I waged battles to protect younger siblings—to get them needed supplies, make them ready for school, take them to church, guard them against predators, and to make my mother understand, "You don't have to go out at night to get Love. I love you."

I fought to get through consequences that weren't mine. I endured being put into foster care and separated from my brothers. I searched for meaning and guidance from the Church. I prayed to God for help.

Finally, I'm broken. At eleven years old, my very sanity hangs in the balance. I surrender any hope of untangling the knot of astonishingly difficult family problems. Only then do I see that I stand alone against unwinnable odds. *Where are my Brothers? Where is the camaraderie? Where did I go wrong?*

#

As the women tell me more about their training, I recall attitudes given to me about the military from my family. One comes from my oldest brother. He enlisted into the Army Reserves and drove a truck. After that he always says, "There's only two types of women in the Army—dykes and whores."

Another attitude comes from early memories of my dad. He tells me stories of what happened to him, his mother, and younger sister in the concentration camp. I'm first generation American and second generation Holocaust survivor on his side. He describes changes his body underwent as he slowly starved . . . the remorse he feels for taking his sister's bread . . . the guilt he suffers for her death. He always ends by saying, "Never trust your government."

Decades later, as I raise my hand and swear an oath to the Constitution, I picture his face. In my mind's ear, I hear his thick Eastern European accent. My heart jumps in my chest. I fear I might betray him. Now, I hope he thinks of me as part of the government—the troops—that liberated the camp and made it possible for him to come to America.

Then I recall my own prejudice about the military. *The military is for losers, for people with no good choices left. It's what you do when you don't know what or how to do anything else.* I realize my error. My generalizations describe only a small portion of the wide body of soldiery. But they sum me up perfectly.

#

Up to this point, I have reinvented and disguised myself many times. I've tried to find my Identity in the church, in New Age groups, in the "American Dream," in helping the handicapped, and in playing amateur sports. Through self-discipline, I've stayed within the rules, boundaries, and expectations for the societal roles I adopt. I develop a chameleon's instinct. I change my colors to clothe myself in the pattern of my surroundings. I call myself by different names and make up fictitious biographies. Every once in a while, I tell someone my real story as if to say, "Do you recognize this? Can you tell me who I am?"

No one ever does. I'm thirty years old and fresh out of ideas for my next incarnation. So I join the military to fit into a ready-made Identity.

What I Learn in Basic Combat Training (BCT)

I LEARN THAT, "HURRY UP and wait," sums up Military Life for the trainee. Daily activities oscillate between vigorous action and periods of sheer boredom.

Hours slow down for trainees on Fire Guard Duty. These same hours pass way too quickly for trainees in their bunks. Such fluctuations erode civilian concepts of Time. The sun, the moon, and the clock on the wall no longer hold sway. Only the drill sergeants' whims pivot the trainees' world.

I learn that a sense of smell belongs to civilian luxury and that camaraderie happens under the strangest conditions. At Reception, we all take note of our bodies' reaction to the Meals Ready to Eat (MREs)—our bowels seize up. On the third day, I walk into the restroom. I smell shit. The odor hits me in the face. I inhale deeply through my nose and say, "Who put the coffee on?" All conversations cease, all faces puzzle, then trainees burst with laughter. Animated chatter devolves along the same crude line. We share the relief of intestinal release. Right then I meet my first friends.

I learn that privacy exists only between my ears. I perform my private body functions, bare-assed, only ten inches away from squad mates as we hold a conversation.

I learn to keep a straight face while being yelled at by a drill sergeant with a lazy eye. Trainees who snicker and crack up become playthings for the drill sergeant's amusement.

I learn my personal space only exists inside my Battle Dress Uniform (BDUs). "Cattle trucks," the Cadillac of Ft. Leonard Wood, arrive to take us from Reception to the Initial Entry Training (IET) area. I cram in alongside other trainees. During the trip, I sympathize with suspended sides of beef.

This confinement affords me some precious time for personal thought. In those brief moments, I think of escape. *Get me of out of this cattle truck! This is the worst!* When the door opens, I'm proven so very wrong. I learn the true meaning of, "No matter how bad it gets, it can always get worse." I exit into a swarm of drill sergeants, the *shakedown*. They buzz about, yelling insults punctuated liberally with swear words. Every command comes fast. Every effort to obey that command never comes fast enough.

I feel sorry for the trainee next to me. She sobs and pleads. She fuels the drill sergeant's tirade. Tears and snot cover her face. Then I recall my lesson from childhood. *Everyone for themselves. Get out if you can.* I stare straight ahead at my duffle bag. I know what's coming. Sure enough, her breakdown draws the attention of two other drill sergeants. They swarm.

The yelling and chaos feel quite familiar, just like home. "Pick it up!" My arms burn as I hold my duffle bag out in front of me. "Put it down!" I follow commands with complete composure. "Pick it up! Put it down! Why did you put that down?" I realize it's not possible to please the drill sergeants. I wait for the frenzy to stop. The senior drill sergeant takes notice of my calm. She sets out to mold me into a leader. She introduces me to my first lesson: that blubbering mess beside me, my first Battle Buddy.

I learn the Army tears down and rebuilds in its own image for its own purposes. "You're a strong person," my senior drill sergeant explains, "but that's not the same as a good leader." She tries to mold me, to make me form an altruistic attachment through a succession of ever more helpless Battle Buddies. Though thirty years of age, I possess no significant connections to the civilian world. No addresses for sending or receiving letters. No phone numbers to call. Nobody sends care-packages. Nobody attends my graduation. The boundaries of my alone-ness finally expose I'm people poor. But I think, *I'm okay. I got away. It's the price I pay to be free.* My alone-ness shadows, pulls, and propels me.

I learn that Military Life suits my self-discipline and morning-person personality. By attaining the highest PT score, I earn the honor to carry the platoon flag. I receive a promotion in rank. I achieve commendations for rifle marksmanship, grenades, and claymore mines. I awaken every morning in anticipation of the platoon run. I really enjoy cadence!

Some lessons belong to the overall arc of my life. Many institutions and their agents play their part. These lessons develop in the far corners of my awareness, beyond vestiges of childhood dreams. One such lesson starts about four weeks into BCT. This lesson reveals one of my deepest character flaws. It puts me square in the crosshairs of Women's Identity in the military and on a collision course with the narcissistic Dr. N.

My Body stops recovering from PT. Every movement feels painful, fatigues. Every effort takes more energy, more focus. Food adds little fuel and constipates. My hair falls out. My skin dries, cracks. I become sensitive to cold, and sluggish. I don't know what to do. So I start showing up at the troop clinic. I want to say, "Tell me what's wrong. Give me some medicine. Fix it. I want to get back to my platoon."

I don't know how to express such a dangerous request. How to tell someone, "I want." How to think they will give-a-shit enough to help. My Personal Code of self-sufficiency states, "If I can't get, do, or learn it on my own, I don't need or want it." My self-discipline allows hesitant acceptance of benign charity for essentials only. Thus my emotional austerity keeps me mobile and unencumbered.

I push my Body. I enjoy intermittent periods of participation. Then in pain, fear, and shame I go to the troop clinic again. The doctor writes another script for "No PT x 3 days." I feel confusion, frustration. *Why don't they try to figure out what's wrong?* Then I realize they don't believe me. They think I'm just trying to get out of PT by faking. This becomes my first exposure to the attitude toward Women's Identity in the military.

So I push my Body the harder. Recalibrate my chameleon self to the cadence call: "Motivated, motivated, Drill Sergeant, reee-al motivated!" I complete the required skills training and graduate BCT. The bus ride to San Antonio, for Advanced Individual Training (AIT), reunites me with my buddies from Reception. I smile until my face hurts, pig out on junk food, and sleep on the bus floor. The sound of wheels moving over pavement soothes me like a lullaby.

What I Learn in AIT

I LEARN THAT THE DRILL sergeants consider me a soldier. They expect possession of BCT skills and performance of a military bearing. No more verbal lashings. Now formal punishment gets meted out.

AIT reintroduces concepts of Time, Personal Space and Choice. I have a schedule with free time that permits travel within the company area. I no longer march everywhere en masse with my platoon.

I learn that drill sergeants really like the word "behoove." I get admonished to *behoove* myself several times a day.

I learn that when someone yells out, "Hey, you!" or "Hey, soldier!" never turn around, keep walking. Let some other sap be a gopher.

Classes in the Army differ from those at a civilian college. If a soldier feels tired, it behooves her to stand in the back of the room—even do push-ups. To fall asleep in class brings swift punishment. My undiagnosed disease causes me to lose consciousness with eyes wide open in class and while I sit for the National EMT exam. Each time I wake up and soldier on. It's the oddest sensation to "come to" like that—after my brain shuts off.

I learn I suck at performing protocols of rank with officers, so I develop a quick-turn avoidance strategy.

"Perception of wrongdoing is the same as being guilty," informs the senior drill sergeant. I learn this as my Body continues to struggle with temperature regulation. It's June in San Antonio with no AC in the barracks and a wool blanket on my bed. One night the senior Drill Sergeant makes rounds with the Fire Guard. He sees me in my bunk— wearing only one set of PT clothes, not the required two sets for females. I don't remember removing my clothes. I say this over and over to no avail. He thunders, roars, and brands me a brazen hussy. I learn there's a first time for everything. I receive a Summarized Article 15. I experience what it feels like to be grounded. The rest of my platoon phases without me for our first weekend pass. I get to police the grounds (pick up trash), polish, clean, and gopher for the Company.

#

My memory feels tattered as I try to piece together the remainder of AIT. I know cool, fun, boring, and miserable stuff happened, but it escapes my re-call. I suspect my spotty memory stems from the disease process and lack of medical treatment. I pull out a folder that stores my Army medical records, Individual Sick Slips, and Medical Care forms. I look at the dates. They show frequent visits to the troop clinic. I look at the summary of symptoms. Each shows the same complaints: fatigue; drowsiness; headaches; edema; dry skin; sensitivity to cold/heat; thin, brittle nails; irregular menstrual cycles; and low-er abdominal, inguinal pain. Again and again, I see the same doctor note in the Remarks section: "No run/jump." Then, I find two reports by Dr. N for GYN exams. Her second report fails to include her diversion from standard medical practice.

#

I remember my frustration mounts each time I leave the clinic. *Why can't they figure out what's wrong?* I scold myself for weakness in seeking help. *Stop being a baby!* I'm spurred by fear each time I report for sick call. I need them to figure out what's wrong. My confusion compounds at the many GYN exams. *Why fixate on my complaint of lower abdominal pain? What does my vagina have to do with it?* After the GYN exam, the doctor looks at me with chagrin as though I removed the toy from the cereal box.

I graduate Combat Medic School (CMS). I move to new barracks—a new Company—and start the next part of my AIT: Practical Nurse. One day I report for Sick Call, and the medic happens to be my bunkmate from CMS. She takes my vitals. I complain of lower abdominal pain, among other things. Once again I prepare for a GYN exam. Dr. N walks into the room. She wears a flight suit. I remember her from a previous GYN exam. *Why does she wear that flight suit?* I chat and catch-up with the medic. Dr. N notices our familiarity and inquires, "Do you know each other?" We both answer in the affirmative. She tells the medic, "You stay. I need a chaperone."

The medic and I share a confused look. It's not procedure for female doctors to use chaperones for GYN exams. The medic obeys the captain's order; she comes back into the room and closes the door. I get into the stirrups and drape with a sheet. The medic stands back across the room and off to my left. Dr. N sits on a stool in front of me, does the digital exam, and places the speculum. I try to zone-out, count the little pockmarks in the ceiling tiles.

I startle when Dr. N suddenly pushes back away from me. I hear the wheels turn and roll on the tile floor. Dr. N jumps to her feet. She points to where she placed the speculum and addresses the medic. "Look! Do you see? There's nothing wrong!"

Before I hear the medic answer, my awareness shifts and takes the perspective of being across the room and to my right. I see the medic make the briefest of glances and nod toward Dr. N to satisfy her order.

I can't move. I'm on display. Legs up. Legs out. The open device inside me pins me down. Dr. N puts her hand behind the medic's head and pushes her toward me across the room and down between my legs. She says, "See? Look! There's nothing wrong!" My breath catches in my throat. I feel shame with my femaleness on display. I see the medic nod her head more vigorously. Dr. N releases her. My mind shuts off.

I remember I'm buttoning my BDU shirt. My hands move in slow motion. *Are these my hands?* They act from automatic, tactile memory. *Feels strange to do something so normal, button-by-button.* My mind shuts off again.

I find myself seated in a chair across from Dr. N's desk. She talks. I don't understand. *Why is she so upset?* She says, "Do yourself and the Military a favor and just get out!" and continues to list the reasons I'm not worth much, not good enough. She talks on and on. My ears rush; they roar with bloody beats. My gut churns her words. The raw shame from the exam digs up all the other times I've felt not good enough. They commandeer my failures. Her words drill, pierce, and pound. They break apart the newly poured foundation of my Identity. Then she gives me a "No run/jump" Sick Slip.

I remember I feel pressure on one foot, then the other. I must be walking. *Faster! Everyone knows. No one must ever know!* I worry I won't finish training or worse, get Recycled. I think about killing myself. Fear advises, *Keep your head down! Keep your mouth shut! Keep moving!*

During the next couple of months, my Body continues to break down. I try to boost my energy and concentration by drinking lots of shots of espresso. I smoke lots of cigarettes. But my grades fall. My PT scores fall. My Body swells and diminishes. One Saturday morning I get ready for formation. I feel so ill, so weak. I think about going to Sick Call. *They will just do another GYN exam and look at me like I'm crazy!* I continue to get ready. Then a clear, calm, compelling voice says, **"But you're dying."** Not one to question "voices from the sky," I go to Sick Call.

The only doctor on duty happens to be a pathologist, a guy who *deals with dead bodies.* Though quite fatigued, I'm not ready for a long nap in a metal drawer. Barely there, without hope and on automatic, I sit up on the exam table and describe my symptoms. As I talk, the doctor slowly backs away. My confidence, already low, vanishes. I think *how odd,* but keep talking.

Suddenly he asks, "Have you ever had your hormones checked?"

I shake my head.

He says he sees, ". . . Myxedema" and orders blood tests.

Next day I get an urgent call from the ER. They diagnose me with Severely Underactive Thyroid (Hypothyroidism). *That's what I needed this whole time—a simple blood test?* All Military Might now bears down on my diagnosis and treatment. Everything moves with a purpose now. They give me a pill at the ER. I report to Dr. K, an endocrinologist. She writes a script for Synthroid, does more blood tests, checks tendon reflexes, and charts my Body's progress. No more shameful "No run/jump" Sick Slips. I'm an injured soldier, recovering. Then I start to ask questions and voice concerns: "How did this happen? What does severe Hypothyroidism, or Myxedema, mean? When will my Body be back to normal? Why am I so easily irritated by temperature, noise, and people? Why is my Mind so sluggish?" I learn that no simple answers exist. Their best guess, my illness is an autoimmune response to cold and stress during BCT. My hair, skin, nails, bowels, muscles, stamina, and cognition might recover in a year's time, but from now on, my blood needs to be tested every six months and I must take a daily pill.

Dr. K says, "Hypothyroidism is associated with mental and mood disorders." I ask her for permission to live off-post while my Body and Mind heal. "The medication isn't going to cure what was already there," she responds. Then she asks, "Do you want to see Psych?"

Alarms bells go off in my Mind. *Keep your head down! Keep your mouth shut! Keep moving! You'll get Recycled through training. I'm not going through this shit again!* I shake my head.

Home Again

I COME HOME. WELL, MY body comes home—home to San Antonio. The term *home* lost its significance for me years ago, if it ever had any. I imagine the incarnation of that word standing on some dirt road, thumb out, with "Show me the way to go home," scrawled on a weather-beaten cardboard sign. Early in my life, I took small comfort in a literal interpretation of the phrase, "Home is where the heart is." *Home* meant my physical pumping, beating, bleeding Heart inside my chest. I come to accept that there's no "Home" for me in this World. I'm a stranger, a sojourner.

But whatever I come back to, I come back quite different, though, to some extent, I expect that. I believe anyone who completes military training comes out, on the other end, fundamentally different. That person will never view the world or herself in the same way. I come away with something missing. As always, my Chameleon Instinct takes hold of that missing something, applies adaptations, tries different blends; each version, one by one, disappears into a perforation inside me—vanishes through me. To my Mind's eye, it looks like a Black Hole, a Super Massive. My Mind's ear hears a cosmologist's depiction of an Event Horizon—the Black Hole's voracious gaping maw. I hear the scientist describe the rapacious devouring of a poor young star.

#

I show up for Drill but feel severely ill. I'm given a Medical Release from the Army Reserves. I pay back my enlistment bonus. I try to move on, chalk it up as another one of my many failures to belong, to find an identity in life. My Chameleon Instinct fits me with mimicry skills. *Put me in any situation, I'll figure it out.*

The Army says, "See one. Do one. Teach one." That used to be my learning curve but not now. I try two different roommate situations that don't work. My moods go to extremes—to outbursts. Sometimes I can't leave my room for days or weeks. I develop a silent treatment that qualifies for the Guinness Book. I try to socialize, hang out, and go to parties. Drinking takes on a bigger role for me. Though I avoid drinking alone, alcohol becomes a necessity for social situations.

I'm not finding a suitable adaptation. There's something different in my Being, some rearrangement, some agent. It supplants my nature and springs a trapdoor over a bottomless, whirling pit. How do I adapt to this thing? It comes out of nowhere, sucks all my energy, disengages cognitive functions, and amps up my nervous system until painful muscle spasms cut into my bones. The debility, so complete, keeps me isolated. Days, weeks pass. I scold myself for being a failure: "Figure this out, already!" Just as suddenly the mood lifts. I pick myself up and try all the harder to keep from falling. But my solitary efforts only amass desperation. I fall so much that I forget not falling.

I seek help from two different VA therapists. They tell me, "The reason Dr. N treated you that way is because you are marked from your childhood." Something in me accepts that. They give me an antidepressant. I experience huge panic attacks. I learn to fear the next one. They give me meds for anxiety.

I try to mimic a normal person, an upstanding citizen. I work hard. I buy a home and a new vehicle. I chat in Internet chat rooms. It's the 1990s. I enjoy an intellectual and emotional expression of pseudo intimacy online. I feel. I laugh. I want to connect, yet much of my emotional landscape remains barren. My computer's power button makes for a clean getaway. I must keep it that way. Keep the area clear—horizon to horizon. Stand. Watch. See it coming this time. I experience intervals of a kind of normality. I furnish my home, join in social events, and go out to Canyon Lake. But without warning, the trapdoor trips, dumps me into the belly of debility. I'm not able to shower or brush my teeth. I can't leave my home or talk on the phone or through the Internet. Racing thoughts, thoughts of suicide, monopolize my Mind as a specter of existential Fear looms over me, nips at me.

The agent of the abyss hides. I try to learn its habits, triggers. *Know your enemy.* It takes liberties with my Mind and emotions, clothes itself in my flesh. It co-opts my memories, tells me, "You've always been this way." I see enemies everywhere. I experience pain everywhere in my Body. I feel a coward for not killing myself. Then I pick myself up. I push. I fall down. I think myself weak and pathetic each time I try and fail. Each fall feels like the end, yet something in me rises. I learn to hate the thing that rises. I learn to loathe it. I blame it for all my failures. *If it didn't raise me up, I wouldn't fall. My problems stem from the rising-thing,* I think. *If I kill the thing that rises, I won't get up, won't fall down.* Soon, killing it is killing me.

I'm alone, but not by myself. Wispy shadows lurk and swirl along the far edges of my peripheral vision. My Mind's ear hears voices that taunt, scream, and implore: *Do yourself and 'Life' a favor and get out.* My Mind forges this bastardized mantra from Dr. N into a weapon. My Body holds the blame, clenches around the shame: *It's because you're weak and marked! That's why Dr. N did it.* A voice whispering, "She's right. Do yourself a favor," causes my Mind to spin, my Heart to race. Then, in full flight, I run. I run out of the house and yard. Arms and legs pump. Chest heaves. Vision narrows. I keep running through the field—beyond the neighborhood. I want to run past city, state, and country. I want to zoom right off the planet. I fall down. Then I see. It's inside me. Even if I rocket to the rings of Saturn, it's inside me. I pick myself up. They give me more meds, different meds.

I dread leaving the house. Outside my door, phantoms lurk. They wait to pounce. I implore my Mind—*they're not real*— but it refuses to accept logic or a quick peek through the blinds. I give in and appease anxiety with a drink, enhance that drink with a pill, and silence my Body with a bowl. In the car I rehearse every moment to come so I appear normal. I go through the motions. I dread the drive back to the house, through the phantom gauntlet. Anxious thoughts pounce as soon as I get into my vehicle. Any experience gets recorded and distorted. My interactions with patients, coworkers, even convenience store and fast food cashiers, are replayed in a constant loop. I learn not to pause playback. It only invites the Critic, who uses shame to erase any good feelings with, *You're marked. You're contagious.* The Critic dubs warnings over any friendly interactions with, *Danger! Keep people away! Do them a favor.*

Alcohol gets me out of the house and back home, albeit to pass out in a black out. I tolerate three days of twelve-hour shifts at work. Then I drink at the bar. Unlike my pre-military drinking, I don't care about two-stepping and socializing. I drink with a purpose. Next morning my Body feels like *the piece of shit that it is.* The Critic greets me before my eyes open. I don't do hangover cures. I keep the pain to pin down the thing that *rises* and to chase Fear away. *I don't have to fear because the pain is already here.*

#

Pain, alcohol, and meds continue as my base coping strategy for many years— fourteen to be exact. I see many doctors. I see many therapists. Always more meds, always more talk. I never question why I'm not receiving help to stop the cycles and give me traction. I assume the therapists know that it was " . . . already there." Everything confirms that I'm " . . . marked."

Not until I get sober do I achieve any real progress at coping. This happens when I finally feel safe enough to fall, stay down, and wait for further instructions. But safe isn't what it feels like at first. It feels like a trap, like I'm backed into a corner. I see three options: increase self-medication (alcohol, pot, and pills); surrender to the voices that say do myself a favor and *get out;* or *run!* Of course I choose *run!* because " . . . going always looks like more fun." I plan to stop paying the mortgage and to save up my cash until the bank forecloses. Then I'll head out to warmer climes. Find an Oasis.

One day, in one of my spins, comes a big panic. My chest tightens, My heart races. I call 911. As one paramedic takes my vitals, another walks through my house. He comes back and says, "Are you wanting to kill yourself?" I don't know what it is about my décor that makes him ask, but the question sticks in my mind. *Do I?* Another day I review my escape plan. A clear, calm, compelling voice says, **"But you can't run. Remember what happened the last time? Are you in any better condition now?"**

I do remember the last time. Nine years earlier, I ran with a much better plan: I'd move from Texas, stay with my brother in northern Indiana, get a place, attend DeVry University near Chicago in the fall, and work for a Travel Nurse Agency. But Life happened and kept happening. The engine blew up in my SUV. I bought a beater car. No apartment complex I called allowed two dogs (what the f*** Illinois). I disagree with my sister-in-law. I move out in the middle of a rainy night. Then my clunker car clunked out. A job isn't much if you can't get to it. Somewhere, some-when, I lost my Chameleon Instinct, the ability, the agility to blend with Life. More drama as I ended up homeless in Indianapolis. Now I answer the voice in my head: "No. I'm not in a better condition. If anything, I will fall down faster."

During one of my several trips to the VA Hospital Psych ward, I get honest about my substance abuse. For the first time I meet someone, a recovering alcoholic. I see something in his eyes, a Light. *I used to have a Light.* I believe him. I must. I'm tired, hollowed out. He makes a plan with me to start treatment. He asks me to commit to the plan. He says, "I'm counting on you." Something in me knows to let him down really means to let me down.

I go home and continue to drink and use drugs. But I show up at treatment on Monday. I stop using alcohol, pills, and pot. Later, when I experience a disc herniation in my neck, a "reservation " for pot surfaces—a justification. *No one can judge you now.* I take my last Start-Over token on February 10th, 2013. My life today amazes me. I think, *Is this really my life?* I'm convinced that substance abuse as a coping strategy only hollowed me out. Though I keep falling down, the depth becomes shallower. Now it's more like stumbling.

Today I release the shame of that most unethical GYN exam. The shame belongs to Dr. N alone. She chose to assault my bunkmate and me with some weird demonstration. She chose to treat me as a malingerer, a trickster. Dr. N chose to ignore the guiding principle of physicians, "First, do no harm." Today I let my life with sobriety get, " . . . a good enough grip on me to make me stay." I work hard at my Program. I keep recovery strategies close with daily practice; make phone calls; maintain a certain simple attitude; do service; and help others through the Steps. I don't play doctor or chemist. I trust the professionals at the VA Hospital. I no longer ". . . stand alone against unwinnable odds." I'm part of a support system.

Some days are better than others, yet over a considerable period of time, the trajectory of my life shows a positive progression. I come across the opportunity to write this memoir after I start training to become a Certified Peer Specialist. Then arrives an offer to become a Peer Specialist for survivors of Military Sexual Trauma (MST), to share my whole story as a survivor of MST recovering from substance abuse and mental health issues. Today I remember I wasn't always falling down. I remember my chameleon instinct, my empathy, my desire for a ". . . kinship bond."

I get a bit sore in the process. I take time to heal. Personal questions still unbalance me. Yet I feel a calling to share the story of my recovery. I hope to inspire others to recover and share until various voices, far-flung perspectives, different experiences, and degrees of bottoms all broadcast, "If I can do it, you can do it."

My Weapons Card

I caress your tactile nature
Between my thumb and forefinger
I feel your diamonds
Rub your crosshatch pattern
Friction against my ridges and whorls
I know you without seeing
In drawers, in pockets, I find you

I keep you to remember my anticipation
Undaunted by standing long
In formation, in silence, in the bone-cold
My eagerness to surrender you, My Weapons Card
I only hold you to allow me to
Procure Her, my weapon
My Hands reach out, grasp powerful Purpose
I hold Her cold metal hard plastic
Reassuring bulk against my Body

I raise Her "Get that weapon up!"
Hold Her there

Shoulders ache while I run in place
I carry, cradle Her to me "Don't drop it!"
Arms burn on miles-long Tactical marches

At the shooting range
I slide Her magazine, click it into position
I hug Her tight to my shoulder
Forefinger snug on Her trigger
Eye-line back and front sights
Exhale and squeeze
Kick-Pop-Bang
Brass ejects and tinkles across the gravel
Something in me smiles

I enjoy the hours I dismantle Her
Warm from my touch, the smell of gun oil
Traces of burnt gunpowder
I caress every part, polish heedless of
The black residue that seeps into and stains
The lines of my fingers

I keep you, My Weapons Card
To remember Her and
To remember that
I'm a trained Soldier
Not a Girl Scout
I'm a Marksman
Lethal, Proficient

Robin Zetka Hall enlisted in the Indiana Army National Guard in 1978 at twenty-four years old. She served over thirty-three years with assignments in the Indiana State Headquarters, the 38th Infantry Division, and the Installation Support Unit at Camp Atterbury. Deployed to Bosnia in 2004, she attained the rank of Chief Warrant Officer Four.

WHERE I'VE BEEN: FROM BOSTON TO BOSNIA

ROBIN HALL

War Games

"BANG, BANG! YOU'RE DEAD, BOBBY."

"No, I'm not. You missed me," he said.

"I did, too, hit you. I got you in the shoulder. . . ."

Behind our Boston row housing and beyond its alley, spread several acres of hilly woods where Bobby and I and the others, ranging in age from four to nine, literally took to the hills to play cowboys and Indians or Army. With Army, we made up teams—the U.S. versus the enemy, often the Germans. I became my favorite TV show character, Sergeant "Chip" Sanders, leading my troops to victory.

I liked to watch *Combat!*, the TV show with Vic Morrow as the star. He was a platoon sergeant who led his guys through small French towns pursuing the Germans during World War II. He was constantly getting into a confrontation with the Germans but always winning in the end. One Christmas, Santa brought me the board game *Combat!*. That's all I played for weeks, until my friends got bored with it all.

On rainy days my friend Chuckie and I lined up our little, green plastic soldiers on his covered porch. He lived downstairs on the first floor of our building, two floors below us. Chuckie lined his soldiers up on one end of the porch, while I positioned mine on the other. We took turns rolling a marble or small ball back and forth, knocking down the enemy in our own little combat scenarios until only one or two soldiers were left standing. The winner got his or her choice of three of the loser's green combatants.

On Saturday mornings all the neighborhood kids rode the trolley into downtown Boston. There we treated ourselves to the latest western, horror, or war movie. Afterwards, we ate two to three Traditional John's Hotdogs for ten cents each. Hamburgers were fifteen cents. Then, till time to go home, we dashed off to the Boston Commons to play more war games in the park.

Uncle Frank

THOUGH MY CHILDHOOD WAS FILLED with games, I couldn't escape growing up. I learned about the Cold War, Vietnam, and the assassinations of John F. Kennedy, Martin Luther King, and Bobby Kennedy. My Uncle Frank, only thirteen years older than me, served in Vietnam in the Air Force. I remember how sharp he looked in his starched uniform. While he served in Vietnam, the family was always on edge when the news told of Air Force personnel being killed. It would be a couple of days before we got word he was okay.

Uncle Frank came home on leave occasionally, and then he'd spend time with me. I always learned some kind of important lesson from him. My first one was not to get shaving cream in my eyes. One morning while he was shaving, I started pestering him by continually pushing the bathroom door open and laughing at him. Catching me off guard, he chased me down the hallway with a handful of shaving cream. When he caught me, he smashed the cream in my face. Problem was, my eyes were not closed. Can you say "sting?" I bawled loud and clear until we got that shaving cream washed out of my eyes. It was Uncle Frank's turn to laugh, and I never bothered him again while he shaved.

Uncle Frank also taught me that if you have a knife in a fight, and you're not careful, it could be taken away and used against you. To prove his point, he handed me a gray rubber knife with a dark brown handle that looked like a Marine K-bar. Thinking I could outwit him, I quickly charged and tried to stab him in the chest. In a flash he had the knife against my throat and one arm wrapped behind my back. After some constructive criticism of my attack, he let me go. Then he taught me how to perform his maneuver and also showed me a better way to attack.

Uncle Frank married a German woman while he was stationed in Germany. As he and Marie started a family, our time together became even less frequent. Uncle Frank didn't make it home for my high school graduation, but he and his family did come to my college graduation. I was thrilled that they could attend.

My relationship with Uncle Frank was the main reason I joined the military, but he wasn't the only family member who'd been in the service. My grandfather had served with the Coast Guard, my father with the Navy, and my cousin Walter with the Marines. I'm sure there were others. I think I was destined to join the military. *It was in the blood,* as they say.

In graduate school I completed a Master's Degree in Physical Education, specializing in Athletic Training. I was also certified as an Emergency Medical Technician. Amusing myself by looking through the want ads one day, I came across an ad to "help your neighbors in times of emergency, floods, etc." That job sounded like a good fit, so I called. I'm sure the look on my face was priceless as the person on the other end answered, "Indiana Army National Guard, Sergeant So-'n-so. How can I help you?"

It seemed like minutes passed before I heard my voice tell him why I called. In a matter of weeks, I had completed all testing, passed the physical, and signed the required paperwork. On 28 December 1978, I was sworn into the military with an April departure date for Basic Training. Because of my advanced education, I immediately attained the rank of Private First Class. And so a new adventure began, not as an EMT, Athletic Trainer, or a teacher but as a heavy-wheeled vehicle mechanic. A strange choice, indeed, or was it?

Basic Training and Then Some

Army Basic Combat Training at Ft. Dix, New Jersey, 1979

WHAT I LEARNED:

- Drill sergeants rule the roost.

- Do what you're told without question; questioning leads to lots of yelling and push-ups.
- Getting multiple inoculations with air guns hurt, but don't flinch or you'll bleed.
- It takes stamina to write your life history on a million different forms that ask the same questions.
- It's imperative to know the Army rank structure and when and who to salute.
- A soldier must take pride in the proper wear of the military uniform.
- There's a correct way to hang clothes in a closet so they are evenly spaced and facing the same direction.
- It's necessary to take care of your feet every day because without them you won't go anywhere.
- It pays to get up before you hear the loud shrill 4 a.m. whistles.
- There's a proper way to perform a military push-up and sit-up, and there are consequences when they aren't done right.
- Drill and ceremony means marching as a unit and other fancy moves to explicit and non-explicit cadence.
- The cadence call "A Yellow Bird" is not my favorite; the vulgarities hurt my ears.
- Cattle cars are not just for cattle or getting to know your battle buddies up close and personal. They actually take you places and get you out of the rain.
- It's possible to eat a whole plate of food in 4.5 minutes with crotchety drill sergeants screaming in your face.
- You must stay awake through first aid classes because you or your buddy will need the information soon.
- Don't drop your weapon or you'll do a million push-ups by graduation.
- You can walk just about anywhere you need to go even if you and your feet don't want to.
- Physical training (PT) is an everyday, all-day-long event you learn to love, because they tell you to.
- I can do more push-ups and sit-ups, run faster, and throw grenades better than a lot of the guys.

- They weren't lying: gas masks only work when properly sealed, and CS gas does burn your eyes and skin.
- When they say 9 *seconds,* they don't mean 9.5 *seconds.*
- The obstacle course is challenging and fun as long as you don't fall off any obstacles, especially the net.
- Marksmanship training starts in the classroom with taking the M-16 rifle apart and putting it back together. (My battle buddy commented, "How come I have extra parts?")
- Don't ever point your weapon anywhere but downrange; drill sergeants get very excited when they are unexpectedly looking down the barrel of your weapon.
- If you can't get your shot group close enough, you may find the drill sergeant's foot stepping on your helmet. (Yes, with your head in it.)
- While the guys play basketball or pool on Sunday afternoons, the ladies throw practice grenades at trashcans. Somehow, that's just not the same.
- Attending church gives you a few hours away from the grind, friendly faces, and a sweet snack.
- Dropping a live grenade definitely gets the drill sergeant's blood pumping and the offender literally thrown to the ground.
- Throwing a live grenade and seeing tractor tires fly through the air is pretty cool.
- Running through the woods during Fire and Maneuver Training is fun and recalls childhood memories of playing Army in the hills behind my home.
- Always keep your feet as dry as possible, and always have an extra pair of dry socks.
- Don't be picky about which C-rations you get. Be glad you finally stopped long enough to eat.
- *Bivouac* is another name for camping out with 120 of your newest best friends, Army style.
- Drill sergeants will harass you in your tent in the middle of the night. In the morning they repeat back to you what you said. Example: My tent mate wakes me and whispers, "There's someone out there. What should we do?" As I'm rolling over, I say, "Go back to sleep." Guess what we heard at breakfast?

- I'm part goat. I can climb a seven-foot wall without assistance. Three male team members that started before me were still pulling each other up to the top when I reached the other side.
- When you reach an obstacle such as a water crossing, take a step back to assess the situation. This will let you think outside the box and not get wet. Long sticks come in handy.
- You don't get to stay inside on cold and rainy days: "Train like you'll fight."
- If you get a chance to take a nap, do it, but don't get caught. Keep your eyes open.
- Trust your training and your battle buddy.
- Take care of those around you. One of them may save your life one day.
- I can always push myself a little harder and do more than I think I can.
- The drill sergeants really do want you to succeed. At graduation you represent their training.

To Weld or Not to Weld

"HERE FIRST SERGEANT!" I YELLED. It was my first drill with the unit after returning from Basic and Advanced Individual Training (AIT). My enlistment papers sent me to Aberdeen Proving Grounds, Maryland, after basic training where I was to be schooled as a welder. In order for me to get into a training spot two months sooner, however, my Military Occupational Specialty (MOS) was changed—with my naive consent—to Heavy Wheel Vehicle Mechanic. The tradeoff was that I would be trained on the job (OJT) as a welder when I returned to my unit from AIT.

So here I stood at attention on a cool September Saturday morning at *oh dark thirty* inside an old flight hangar, part of the old Cox Municipal Airport, now known as Stout Field. My group, the Service Support Platoon, stood at the end of the formation uniformly clad in our olive-drab pickle suits and spit-shined black boots. Our unit designation was Company F-Heavy Maintenance, 738th Maintenance Battalion, 38th Infantry Division. Company F was one of the largest units, with over 200 soldiers, but I was one of only two women in the entire company. The other female worked in the Shop Office. Hers was a desk job but still an important cog in the wheel of Army maintenance. Another woman joined our ranks months later working in the Armament Section.

The other welder in the section was my first line supervisor, Sergeant Mullins. He was in his mid-twenties, an easy-going, free spirit with a good sense of humor. He could be counted on for silly comments, but he always accomplished the mission. All the guys were friendly and looked out for me. It was like working with a bunch of big brothers.

It seemed like all we did the first several months was inventory and inspections—so much for OJT as a welder. We would sit in the welder's van, a two-and-a-half-ton truck with work benches and storage compartments, doing our inventories and talking about current events: Margaret Thatcher's election as the first female Prime Minister of England, the USSR's invasion of Afghanistan and the controversy over whether the U.S. would get involved, Jim Jones and the People's Temple in Guyana, and the debate as to whether we should eat lunch with the unit or go to McDonald's or Wendy's.

Staff Sergeant Gibson, the platoon sergeant, would sometimes pull me aside to help him with paperwork. At first I thought he was pulling me out because I was a woman, but in reality it was to help me better understand the process of getting repairs done. He wanted me to become eligible for better opportunities, to move up in rank when the time came.

I discovered all the inventory and inspections were in preparation for next year's Annual Training (AT). Prior to AT our unit would undergo a Command Inspection by the division commander (DC). The day before the general's inspection, we practiced proper formations and mastered movements for when he would walk through the ranks. When the big day came and the DC arrived, the unit came to Attention and then to Parade Rest, a modified position of Attention, which is easier to hold for long periods. Hardly a sound could be heard on the massive concrete drill floor. The DC slowly snaked through the ranks of each platoon. The only sounds were muffled voices, an occasional chuckle or cough, and platoon leaders calling their platoons to Attention as the DC approached them and then to Parade Rest when he moved to the next platoon.

Finally, our turn came. We snapped to attention on command. The company commander, executive officer (XO), and platoon leader followed the DC as he went from soldier to soldier. The DC briefly spoke to each and every soldier, asking what sounded like technical questions, as he moved closer to me. This would be the first time I came face to face with a general. I noticed a light sweat in my palms as he moved even closer.

I didn't have a clue as to what he would say or ask, and I hoped I could answer his questions. As the DC stood in front of the guy next to me, I heard him ask where he was from and what his job was. Then he turned and stepped in front of me. Of all things, he said, "So you're the welder?" He caught me off guard, but I replied "Yes, sir," thinking he really meant "the female welder." "Good," he said, "I'll see you at AT." At that he moved on to the next soldier and left me in a quandary. "Wonder what he meant by that?" I thought. Even the company commander had a funny look on his face when he heard the DC's statement.

A few weeks later, during field exercises at AT in Camp Grayling, Michigan, I was outside the welding van when the DC and his entourage came strolling into our area. He walked past my supervisor and several others and right up to me. Looking around, I noticed that other soldiers in the area stopped what they were doing; their eyes were on the general. His staff of four officers circled around behind him—a quizzical look in their eyes. I didn't even have time to salute.

"Told you I'd be coming to see you," he said with a smile. "I need this fixed," and he handed me a small metal box. It was an old, silver lighter with a faded black symbol on it. Obviously, it was something he cherished. The lid came off in my hand when I opened it.

Now, remember, my OJT had yet to happen, so I didn't have any welding training. I glanced over his shoulder at my sergeant who nodded his head. I told the general I'd see what I could do.

Sergeant Mullins and I stepped up into the van. I looked at him with a questioning expression, not knowing what to do. He took the lighter, wrapped it in a small cotton shop rag to protect it and jammed it in the vice, saying, "This type of metal can't be welded."

Great, I thought, *my first job is for the general, and he's telling me it can't be welded.* The sergeant pulled out a soldering gun and a piece of thin wire. It took three hands, but between the two of us we managed to solder the smaller top piece back to the main body of the lighter and still be able to close and open it. Gingerly holding the lighter, I stepped out of the van and handed it back to the

DC. I told him I didn't know how long it would hold.

He took it, opened it, closed it, smiled, said, "Thanks," and departed. I doubt the lighter lasted more than a few times being opened, but for the moment the DC was happy.

Even though I didn't actually repair the lighter, I felt I had learned something about my job. We completed a couple more repairs during that AT. Now I could at least hook up the hoses and light the welding torch, which gave me some satisfaction in regards to my chosen MOS.

Even though I still couldn't weld very well, by the end of AT I felt like part of the service section and well accepted by my male peers. How did I know I was accepted? End of AT activities included a careful cleanup of all the areas and buildings. I was assigned to drive a Jeep with a pallet attached to the back to smooth the sand around several buildings. Grayling is all sand, and we needed to groom the area. While I was dragging the pallet around the last building, a couple of the men came up and stopped me. I noticed several other soldiers in the area were watching and chuckling. I suddenly realized what was on their minds. My grip on the slick steering wheel tightened as I remembered the stories. It was the tradition that all first-timers to Grayling get thrown into Lake Margarethe, a lake ice-cold even in summer.

The trick was to wait till the newbie has his or her last clean uniform on and everything else packed up. As they grabbed my arms, I clenched my hands to the steering wheel so hard they turned frosty white from lack of blood flow. My feet and legs were wedged as best as they could be under the dashboard. I was immovable, as if super-glued in place. My mind was made up: they were not throwing me in the lake! I have a natural aversion to cold water and get really irritated when I get wet unexpectedly. I drew strength from remembering the time in college when four girls from my basketball team tried to push me into a cold shower as a senior rite of passage. That didn't happen, so I wasn't about to let two guys throw me into the lake. I spotted the platoon sergeant in the distance. He appeared to be laughing. He must have thought it was pretty funny that the guys couldn't get me out of the Jeep and had to give up.

I learned a modest amount of welding and soldering and participated in soldiering skills like digging foxholes and guard duty, but I never did experience the Camp Grayling baptism.

Broken Leather

WHEN I ARRIVED AT THE Camp Atterbury horse barn early one morning in late May, several soldiers were already there and had four black beauties hooked up to the practice caisson. As part of the Indiana National Guard Ceremonial Unit, we were preparing for the annual Memorial Day ceremony in Indianapolis. The Caisson Platoon, my section, would carry a mock flag-draped casket on a wagon called a caisson pulled by four horses as part of the procession. Customarily, we would meet at the barn and practice a few days before the event.

Black leather straps were strung along each horse and over their backs, connecting them to the practice caisson. Each of the horses was tethered to a soldier by a long blue lead rope. Normally there are two riders on the left side, but they weren't mounted and held lead lines instead. As I walked toward the group, I noticed the bristling horses in harness seemed a bit restless, occasionally stomping their feet. I also noticed they only had halters on—no bit and bridle.

I'd been platoon leader for only a few months, but I had been with the Caisson Platoon about two years so I had experience with horses, though I wasn't an expert by any means. Knowing the bridle is what controls the horse, I didn't have a good feeling about the situation. I knew several of the guys had horses of their own and were veterans of the Caisson Platoon. Their years of experience with horses gave me some reassurance, yet something inside of me just wasn't at ease.

Playing the naïve and inexperienced female lieutenant, I greeted the group of guys and nonchalantly said, "You know, they only have halters on, are you going to put on their bridles?"

"Yeah, we know," Sergeant "Sayer" said with the voice of experience and confidence. "They'll be just fine." He told me they would walk the horses around the barn a time or two to ensure they were pulling in unison. Then they would put the bridles on the horses and walk down the road. Knowing one of the horses had not pulled with this team before, I looked at the sergeant with concern and asked, "Are you sure?"

He nodded, turned, and plodded over to where the soldiers and horses anxiously stood, ready to step off.

As I headed back to my vehicle, I heard the sergeant give the order to move. I turned and saw, as if in slow motion, all hell break loose. Horses reared and ran in four different directions. The front of the caisson was heaved up into the air and landed on the unforgiving ground, wheels somehow unbroken. One soldier instinctively wrapped his arms around his horse's neck and pulled his feet up to keep from getting trampled and held on for at least fifty yards before the animal finally stopped. Another soldier let go of the lead rope after several running steps and dove to the side, avoiding a thousand pounds of crushing hooves. I didn't see what happened to the other two soldiers. Fortunately, everyone seemed unhurt and already on the move to grab the lead lines of the other three horses that were now grazing on some clumps of grass.

The main shaft of the caisson was broken in two pieces with one piece lying on the ground several feet away. Black leather fragments were strewn everywhere, some straps still attached to the caisson, while other lengths of leather were hanging from each horse. I threw my notebook onto the car and sprinted back towards them.

"Well, shit, I didn't expect that," said Sergeant Sayer. "Is everyone okay?" Thank God, everyone was okay—a few bumps but no major injuries, only some damaged pride. After examining the horses for injuries, we found a couple of scratches on two of them; otherwise, they were just a little rattled.

For the next ten to fifteen minutes everyone gave recollections of what occurred. The assessments gave me a better understanding of what transpired so I could explain later to the leadership. The burning question in my mind was whether bits and bridles would have made a difference. But asking that aloud was the same as saying, "I told you so." So I bit my tongue. I thought better of rubbing salt in the wounds of guys that knew they made a mistake. After all, they were the ones that had to fix the resulting mess.

I had an event meeting in Indianapolis in an hour and a half. Before I left we discussed our way forward as the ceremony was in two days. I needed quick answers as to whether or not we could put together a team of horses that would pull the caisson and whether enough leather could be repaired. With our time constraints, it was decided enough leather could definitely be repaired for a two-horse team, but for all four, it would take a miracle. More importantly, we weren't sure we could get all four horses to work together in such a short time even if all the leather was mended. Our recommended course of action was to go with a two-horse team.

Jumping into my vehicle to head north for the meeting, my mind was a whirl of questions: *How do I explain what happened? And why it happened? What impact will this have on the event? What's the effect on the rest of the Ceremonial Unit if we can't put a pulling team together? Ugh! The Commander won't be happy.*

To make matters worse, on my way to the meeting, I ran into Lieutenant Colonel "Torque." I dreaded telling him what happened with the horses, but as second in charge, he needed to know.

After explaining the situation, I could see the gears turning in his head as he grasped the situation. His dark eyes and ruddy face were only offset by the tone of his voice and his index finger shaking inches from my face as he said sternly, "Lieutenant, you have less than forty-eight hours to get all the leather and harness fixed! If you have to work those hours straight, I expect you to get it done!" My stomach was in knots and my hands were sweaty. Though I had worked with him before, I had not seen this side of him. Then he added, "Representatives from the Old Guard will be here to observe the unit. We have to look good!" As I perceived the gravity of that statement, my knots crept up to my chest.

"Sir, with all due respect, that's not going to happen," I said. "Even if we get the harness and leather repaired, the horses haven't been worked all winter. And one of the horses hasn't pulled with the team before, which is what caused the problem. We can use a two-horse team. If we try to use four and they don't work as a team, the same thing could happen again during the ceremony. I'm more concerned with all the civilians that will be there watching; if the horses go haywire again, people may get hurt."

He just glared at me, as if to say "How dare you not follow my orders!" Being a pretty laid-back person, I think I caught him off guard with my sudden comeback. Turning sharply towards his vehicle, he shouted over his shoulder, "Take it up with Colonel Wrench!" Then he plopped in his truck and drove off towards the meeting.

Colonel "Wrench" was Commander of the Indiana National Guard Ceremonial Unit, sister unit to the Old Guard in Washington, D.C. The whole unit, made up of several sections, was involved in the day's events. All members were volunteers as this was an additional duty.

After I told Colonel Wrench what happened, he wasn't happy, but he completely understood the situation and agreed with me that safety had to come first. A two-horse team was better than none at all. During the ceremony, the team looked strange to us, since it wasn't a four-horse team—but it worked.

The mission was completed. No one got hurt. Most onlookers and civilians probably didn't notice the difference. And the Old Guard visitors totally understood as they had known such accidents at Arlington National Cemetery.

I laugh now when I think of this calamity, envisioning it as a comic strip, frame by frame: caisson and leather flying through the air . . . soldiers hanging on for dear life . . . the lieutenant colonel wagging his finger and barking orders. In retrospect, I should have ensured the soldiers did the right thing—that they put bits and bridles on the horses. I'm sure my guilt in not doing that bolstered my courage to stand up to Lieutenant Colonel Torque.

That catastrophe helped me grow in confidence as a young female officer. The situation with Lieutenant Colonel was the first time in my military career that I stepped out of my comfort zone and stood up to a senior officer. And it wouldn't be the last.

Day Is Done

Adorned with silver spurs,
tall black boots in stirrups reflect
golden handles on polished walnut
snugly wrapped in stripes woven with stars,
accompanied by bearers in blue.
Horses joined in creaking leather turn wheels,
as hooves pound out memories and
blank faces step to drums' somber dirge.
Quiet rustle of the wind broken by
three sharp volleys of seven.
A reverent silence envelops
the bugler's haunting call.

Across the Pond

I THOUGHT I WOULD PEE my pants, turn into a Popsicle, and fall over dead before the drug-sniffing dogs finished inspecting our duffle bags lined up on the tarmac. After a month of training in Hoenfelds, Germany, we had left in a near snowstorm and just off-loaded from a C-130 at Tuzla Airfield, Eagle Base, in Bosnia-Herzegovina. It was a blustery, snowy day with temps in the low twenties. Our group of seventy-five soldiers was the first group to arrive. We were the advance party of the 38th Infantry Division of Indiana National Guard, part of Task Force Eagle. Now we were standing in formation, watching and waiting—waiting for the dogs to finish their work before we could enter the sanctuary of warmth, before any of us could use the bathroom. We were here to replace another unit in the ongoing peacekeeping mission afforded by the Dayton Peace Accord signed in 1995. We would be known as SFOR-15 (Stabilization Force-15th rotation), the last large U.S. peacekeeping force in Bosnia.

Finally, the sergeant approached us and called, "Attention! Right Face. File from the Left." We were directed single file to the large, simple, wooden structure that would later serve as our movie theater. We walked with quick, short strides. My first stop was the restroom. It was a clean multi-seater and warm. My nearly frozen hands had trouble with my belt buckle and my frozen butt could hardly feel the seat, but finally—relief!

Corralled inside the building, we sat in long rows of metal folding chairs, thawing and trying to stay awake. Half-heartedly, we listened to four hours of required briefings and tried to snooze without being noticed. None of this was new. We heard these "death-by-PowerPoint" sermons at least twice over the last few weeks. But they were still required upon entering the country. So we endured.

Then we were introduced to the counterparts we were replacing. They were part of the 34th Infantry Division, a National Guard unit from Minnesota, known as the Red Bulls. Our eight-person section was replacing a group of fourteen. They helped gather our gear and escorted us to our living quarters for the next nine months.

We trained with them for two weeks. The first week they schooled us in the duties we would perform. They were a wealth of information and took us on tours around Eagle Base and to Butmir Base in Sarajevo, introducing us to places and people we would encounter on our own once they departed.

The second week they observed us and gave advice as we took over all their tasks. As the Personnel Services Section, we were responsible for personnel records for all U.S. soldiers on base, military ID cards, and country specific ID cards for soldiers, DOD civilians, and nationals working on base. One of my tasks was ensuring accountability and security of all unused ID cards on hand at Eagle Base and two other outlying bases. I learned to interact with NATO forces from Turkey and Poland. Our language differences weren't too much of an issue as the people I dealt with could speak and understand enough English so that we could communicate. After the Red Bulls left, it didn't take long to fall into the battle rhythm of our mission at Eagle Base.

Working in an office environment most days, I looked forward to getting off base once in a while. A few months into our deployment, I received a call from the Turkish lieutenant that was in charge of the ID cards for his base. He was having problems with the ID card system. I had Specialist Stanback check if the daily helicopter flight to Sarajevo could drop us off at the Turkish base on their way down and pick us up on their way back.

While Spc. Stanback dozed, I relaxed. The whir of the blades put me in Zen mode. . . . Idyllic scenery floated by. . . . I returned to reality in time to see the mountains on the outskirts of Sarajevo. I tapped Spc. Stanback on the leg. He looked over at me as I pointed out the window. The pilots evidently forgot to make the stop at the Turkish base, as Sarajevo was just over the mountains.

After the chopper shut down, we exited. I confronted the pilot, "Chief, you were supposed to drop us off at the Turkish base."

He looked at me kind of funny and said, "No, we weren't."

I countered with, "Yes, you were. Can you call Flight Operations and check?"

He walked to the other side of the helicopter and got on the radio. Shortly, he came back and said, "You're correct. The good news is that we have to return to Eagle Base to pick up some maintenance parts. We can drop you off on the way back and pick you up later."

On the chopper again we headed back over the mountains. It wasn't long until we were approaching the Turkish base. We circled a couple of times so the pilot could pick out a landing spot. As the chopper was getting closer to landing, I noticed several Turks running from the dirt parking lot towards a large building.

As the chopper got closer to the ground, the rotor wash from the blades stirred up a dust storm that enveloped the helicopter. *How does he know how close to the ground he is?* I wondered when suddenly the chopper pitched forward and lurched up and out of the dirt cloud. This maneuver planted my butt firmly in the webbed seating.

I turned to look at Spc. Stanback. I think we both had the same look of apprehension on our faces. The pilot circled around again and found a more suitable landing spot in a grassy area. I don't know about the crew, but the concerned passengers were glad to be on the ground safely. The pilot informed me they would wait for us instead of making a return trip.

A Turkish sergeant scooped us up in a small truck and transported us to the main building where his lieutenant met us. After greeting us, the lieutenant asked that we tell the pilot to call their base before attempting to land there again. I assured him I would.

Though the lieutenant's English was somewhat broken, we managed to fix the problem with his ID card system and accounted for all his cards. We were ready to leave when he invited us for lunch. I started to decline, "Thank you, but the pilots are . . . . " But, remembering our cultural training, I stopped midsentence. "Yes, we'll join you for lunch, but we can't stay long." The pilots would have to wait. I wasn't going to risk insulting my new acquaintance.

The lieutenant escorted us to their dining facility, and we got in line. Having never eaten Turkish food, I had no idea what to expect. The first section was a typical small salad bar, with greens and a few veggies. As I moved on, there were only a few selections. Nothing like what we enjoyed at our dining facility. I took some pasta salad and some marinated vegetables. Next came the fish: a pan of fifteen to twenty whole fish with eyes staring at me. I retraced my steps and took more pasta and veggies. Spc. Stanback tried the fish. He dished it onto his plate and touched it with his finger. It was then that we realized all the food was cold, including the fish.

We sat at the table with the lieutenant and a couple of his soldiers and conversed the best we could. The language barriers and not having much in common limited the conversation to our families. We showed each other pictures and talked about how long it would be before each of us would go home. Stanback said the fish was good, so I tasted it. It was okay, just not what I was used to. I chalked it up to another new experience.

Within thirty minutes, we were saying our goodbyes and offering our future assistance at any time. Our hosts were very gracious. Heading back to the helicopter, I was thankful we stayed for lunch and spent a little time with the Turkish soldiers. I've eaten Turkish food since being home, and it was nothing like my experience in Bosnia; it was much better, with more choices.

In retrospect, my visit gave me a different perspective—one that opened my eyes to how soldiers of another country live while away from home and the difficulty of language barriers.

Scattered Reflections on Bosnia

WHEN I FIRST HEARD I would be deployed to a war-torn country, I was concerned. Several friends were called up at the same time for Afghanistan. I was afraid for all of us. It wasn't a matter of if you would get the call, but rather when and where you would go. Compared to Afghanistan and Iraq, Bosnia didn't sound so bad. We were to be peacekeepers and not necessarily warriors.

Leaving family, friends, and school behind for almost a year was not in my plans. But as a soldier, war is what we train for; it's what we do. I soon learned that Bosnia is a country about the size of West Virginia, with similar weather patterns and landscape. It's a beautiful country, with pastoral hillsides, farmland, villages, and large cities. But war had left its scars on the countryside and the hearts of its people.

I remember the acrid stench in the air when we first arrived in March. We were told the country was economically poor, so much so that people would burn whatever they could to heat their homes in winter—any form of wood, including furniture, and even feces if necessary. Somehow the words didn't sink in until I saw an old woman in an open field strewn with trash and two small piles of sawdust. She was filling five-gallon pails with the sawdust, undoubtedly to heat her home. I wondered if there are people in the U.S. who live this way. I pictured the homeless on the streets of Indianapolis and other cities as well as Native Americans on some reservations.

We were warned not to engage with the gypsies in Sarajevo. These were poor people with no job, who would panhandle or do unrequested odd jobs then expect money. One time we were on our way into town when a young mother in her early twenties, wearing a faded pastel wrap-type dress and headscarf, came up to our van at a stoplight. She was holding a sleeping baby, about two months old, wrapped in a white cloth. The van windows were up, so with a sad face she pointed to us then to her baby, and then put her hand out for money. It broke my heart, but we couldn't do anything.

We were told the gypsies target anyone in military uniform, especially U.S. personnel. Another time, at a red light, two teenage boys wearing raggedy clothes ran out to our van and started washing the windshield. We tried to wave them off, saying, "No!" But they finished the job and then wanted money. When we didn't give them anything, they flipped us off and walked away cussing. Jobs were hard to come by. I felt bad for the people trying to get by the best way they knew how.

These people were in direct contrast to the locals that were able to work on the American bases. The locals were a hardworking group, eager to work and happy to have decent paying jobs. I interacted mostly with the lady who cleaned our building. Language was a big barrier, but she would come in and teach us Americans a word or two of Bosnian each week and we'd teach her some English. She shared pictures of her family, especially her recent grandchild. She was a sweet, funny lady. I gave her an Indiana T-shirt before we left. It made her smile, but her tears were indicative of her uncertain future employment once we left.

The hillsides and rivers were strewn with trash—household appliances, debris from bombed out buildings, and old automobile carcasses. The once-beautiful landscape had been transformed into a universal dumping ground, an ecological atrocity. Every road we drove down had remnants of homesteads with artillery or mortar shell holes in the partial walls that still stood as reminders of the war. Some of the small villages revealed an interesting disparity: a rebuilt and brightly painted home would stand adjacent to a gray house, pock-holed from past attacks.

"Don't step on the grass!" "Be aware of mines!" These were common mantras I heard during my deployment. Signs made of red triangular metal with skull and cross bones and the word MINE hung on trees and posts. They were a constant reminder of the daily dangers of living in Bosnia. Some grassy areas on base were deemed safe from mines. But trekking through any other patches wasn't worth the gamble. I walked on the sports field on base, but, other than that, I didn't step foot on green grass until I got home.

Over two million mines were placed in Bosnia during the wars. Almost a million were still in the ground when we left. One day I was on a bus in Sarajevo that was detoured for construction. At a red light, I looked down at the grassy area between the road and the sidewalk. Just a few feet from my window, yellow tape marked off a forty-foot-long area. Several ten to twelve-inch diameter holes were evenly spaced along it. Each hole represented a mine recently removed. It boggled my mind to think of these mines in the middle of a large city—along a sidewalk traveled daily by hundreds of people.

On occasion we had business at the U.S. Embassy in Sarajevo, but instead of flying down on the daily shuttle, sometimes an NCO and I would drive down. The main roads were very narrow, especially through the mountains—one-car width in places—and very curvy and pothole ridden. We never knew what might appear around the next corner. It could be an oncoming truck or a herd of sheep in the middle of the road. Between mines and crappy roads, the trip to Sarajevo made for a long, arduous drive.

During a tour of the city, we were told how the library was destroyed—all the books were thrown into the middle of the building and burned. The stone structure was boarded up now so you couldn't see inside. It was a humid eighty degrees, but when our group walked by the library's main entrance, an ice-cold breeze blew out from under the plywood boards. That breeze initially felt good in the heat. But I think that as we looked at each other we all felt the same weird sensation. The cold wind coming from that building was just not natural.

Driving through Sarajevo, one saw constant reminders of the atrocities of war. The 1984 Olympic stadium, once a place of athletic endeavor amidst the snow-covered mountains, became the site for a morgue during the war. Now the word *Olympic* was still visible in the seating area, but the massive concrete stadium was gray and run down.

Several cemeteries within the city were so large they seemed to take over whole neighborhoods. Their white stone memorials aligned across rolling hills reminded me of Arlington National Cemetery. These cemeteries contrasted greatly with the smaller churchyards of outlying areas that might have a dozen or so grave markers.

Though my time in Bosnia was brief and my travels within the country were not extensive, I saw enough to appreciate the hidden beauty of the country— in both the people and the countryside. My memories of this war-torn land make me thankful for what we have in our country and grateful for family and friends.

My Helmet

I WORE YOU OFTEN, MY "steel pot," my first helmet, hard and heavy on my head. You were an icon from World War ll and Vietnam. Your cold hard steel was covered with camouflage cloth. A chinstrap held you tight. Inside your strong steel a removable hard hat with webbing made you fit just right. You were one of my battle buddies traveling with me wherever I went—from the sands of Fort Dix, New Jersey, and Camp Grayling, Michigan, to the muddy fields and woods of Camp Atterbury, Indiana. During field exercises you were multi-functional. I often used you as a seat, and with liner removed, you became a washbasin, a bucket, a hammer, and even an entrenching tool. I watched as others even used you as a cook pot. You protected my head from hazards of duty for a few years before you went back to the supply room in the mid-eighties.

You were upgraded to a stronger, lighter, new style, but much of your versatility was lost. This version of you traversed the blue Atlantic with me for training in Germany, then on to Bosnia-Herzegovina as a peacekeeper. Shortly thereafter I turned you in for the last time.

These days, when I see you on soldiers, I remember our training during field exercises and on the range, in the heat of summer and the cold of winter. I wouldn't change those times for anything, and I'm thankful for the protection. But, helmet, *my helmet,* I don't miss your weight on my head.

Letters

HALFWAY THROUGH MY DEPLOYMENT TO Bosnia, I was getting a little homesick and feeling down. I had received a few cards and gifts that included books and curtains from my friend Alice; large bags of my favorite snack, dried cranberries (Craisins), from two different churches that were supporting me with prayer; a present from the women's ministry at my home church; and several pictures of grandkids and other family members. The treasured cards and pictures took up residence on a wall in my connex apartment as a reminder of why I remained a soldier.

One day our young private came back from the mailroom and walked into my office. He held out a large, thick, yellow envelope with a green customs sticker on it. I must have had a puzzled look on my face as I said, "For me? Are you sure?" I usually didn't get much mail.

"Yes, Ma'am, it's got your name on it," he said chuckling. The return address was Franklin, Indiana. And the customs declaration form read, "Letters from Students." My friend Karla was a fourth grade teacher at Indian Creek Elementary School in Trafalgar. She had each of her students write a brief letter to me.

Each letter was in its own small envelope addressed to me with the student's home address in the upper-left corner. I assumed that this project taught students how to properly address and write a letter. At the same time, it allowed them to encourage a soldier. It was hard not to read my letters all in one sitting, but I decided to break the twenty letters into groups of four to extend the excitement. I read four letters each of the next five days. All of the letters were written on standard-lined notebook paper with the familiar gray of a No.2 pencil.

Each letter was a little different, but most students said they liked their teacher, they were ready for summer vacation only weeks away, and they were sad that I was so far from home. Other students told me about their dog or cat, their siblings or friends, and what they were studying in school. A few told more personal stories of home life or a relative who was in the war. I felt a definite connection with them. Several were concerned for my safety, hoping I didn't get shot and that I would be home soon. Their sentiment touched my heart and brought tears to my eyes. I decided to send each student a special postcard from Bosnia to thank them for taking the time to write to me and for their encouragement.

It's been over twelve years now, but I still read those letters every once in a while as a keepsake of where I've been; a reminder that written letters often have more meaning than an email or text; and that even young hearts are emotionally affected by war. These letters still hold a special place in my heart and remind me how important people are in my life.

Depression's Battle

Navigating an uphill path
in a valley of great darkness,
I'm swallowed whole by a mucked up
foxhole of invasive thoughts.
I maneuver through the River of Sorrow,
sleepless nights crowded with memories,
cross fields strewn with
anxiety's tangled roots.

My heart pounds with
senses on edge, vigilant, ready.
Drops of sweat taste bitter
on my tongue.
My shattered soul takes aim at
shadowy figures of past betrayal,
struggling to break the chains
of emotional bondage.
Slowly ascending, reaching
an outstretched hand of hope,
I push back the darkness
and discover a stronger me.

Post-Military Conflict

IN FEBRUARY 2011, I HAD been on active duty at Camp Atterbury for just over three years, working as a Contracting Officer Representative on a multi-million-dollar contract and several smaller contracts. My work kept me busy as I was dealing with multiple contract issues at any given time. Other than the long hours, I enjoyed my job and its social interactions.

Then in March my brother Darrell passed away at the age of fifty after a bizarre event. By August I realized I was on the verge of burn out. The long hours and tedious work were taking their toll. At times, my memory and concentration became almost non-existent. I even argued with a sergeant about a discussion we had a week earlier. He said I had agreed to a particular course of action. I told him I definitely agreed to no such thing. He was not happy when he left my office. A few days later, when I remembered the conversation, I had to eat my words. He had been right.

By then I was spending more time with the massage therapist and chiropractor than I had in quite a while. My back and shoulders were stiff as concrete. I wasn't sleeping well most nights. I feared my ability to make decisions would be next on the list of losses. My body had been rebelling mentally and physically for some time, but now I started listening. My career covered almost thirty-three years at this point, but the last four years had taken their toll. It was time to bow out and begin taking better care of myself. I made the difficult decision to retire in April 2012.

My husband Chuck and I sat down and figured out that for the last ten years one of us had always been on active duty. One of those years I was in Bosnia. He hadn't liked the fact that I went overseas. He thought it should have been him. The geographic separation was difficult for both of us.

Even though we lived in the same house, one or the other of us worked long hours, oftentimes six and seven days a week. For six of those ten years we saw very little of each other. Frequently, one or both of us missed family events and holidays due to mission requirements, something not uncommon in the military. We had become somewhat distant emotionally, with work, eat, and sleep the norm. The time had arrived for us to reconnect. I took four months off before returning to my civilian job.

In July 2012, I resumed my civilian job as an Environmental Specialist. Since this was at Camp Atterbury, I basically moved to the other end of the street. I found the transition somewhat difficult. There had been personnel changes, a new boss, and some alterations in my job requirements. The job changes would lead to an upgrade in position and pay, but I had trouble wrapping my mind and heart around them and eventually relinquished my position.

My transition from the military was not going as planned.

I thought the added stress of the new job was wearing on me. By August I was once again having trouble sleeping, getting only two hours per night if I was lucky. This went on for weeks. Sleep was all I could think about. Finally, I decided I needed medical intervention; my body, mind, and spirit were suffering.

The doctor diagnosed situational depression. Our discussion revolved around Darrell's death the previous year and the recent death of my thirteen-year-old dog. These events along with the emotional separation from my husband, military retirement, and the stress of the current job change—all major life changes—had finally broken me. The next two nights I slept a deep, much-needed sleep. I felt so much better, but my ordeal wasn't over. Now that I felt better I was in denial. Depression wasn't to blame—I just needed more sleep.

Several months later, I responded to a flyer in the elevator at the VA and signed up for an art therapy class. I had no idea what I was getting myself into. I disregarded the word "therapy." I just wanted to do some art.

The class was part of a research grant that studied the use of art therapy for veterans with PTSD, depression, and other related problems. I was still in denial but enjoyed the mindfulness meditation that started and ended each class, along with our various art projects. It intrigued me that my art could say so much about what was stored in the depths of my unconscious brain. My classmates and I shared our thoughts behind the artwork and supported each other through difficult personal feelings and memories. My own artwork resurrected a childhood trauma, but I would not talk about it.

By the end of the second eight-week session, the art therapist asked me some difficult questions about my last drawing: a human stick figure under a tree. He represented my brother. Tears came to my eyes. I finally realized I had unresolved grief regarding his sudden death. Jumping back into my mission at Atterbury after his death, I pushed all the grief behind a secure brick wall in my mind. *A safe place,* I thought. But it was the same place my childhood trauma, guilt, and other unwanted memories resided.

After some serious thought, I pursued professional help for my unresolved grief and what turned out to be a mild form of PTSD and depression. It was hard to accept that I had fallen from *normalcy,* whatever that really means, into the stigma of mental illness. It's a stigma that keeps many people from seeking help because they don't want to be seen as weak or looked at as being different. I would have nothing of that. I wanted my life back. I was willing to do whatever it was to get back to enjoying life.

During my first months of individual counseling, I learned that chronic pain could cause and/or aggravate depression. We also discussed grief and sexual harassment and assault, all of which hold the mind hostage. I'm sure the counselor was frustrated with me at times, having to drag information out of me. As most people can attest, I'm not a talker.

Soon I joined a women's talk therapy group, which I found very supportive. But I also sought out anything that might help in the healing process: Yoga, Tai Chi, mindfulness-based meditation, a group called the Shattered Soul, and anything that resembled art therapy. Art seemed to help the most.

Art allowed me to escape from pain and anxiety for periods of time. I could focus on something other than my problems and put energy into creating for the sake of creating. It was a way of letting my stuffed-in feelings out so I could move forward. I learned to dig into my buried thoughts and feelings.

Eventually I started breaking down that brick wall I built. I faced the shame and guilt of past events and wrongdoings. I faced up to *should-a, would-a, could-a* and understood there's no sense in looking back at what I can't change. I faced my fears of what might happen but usually doesn't. I learned about forgiveness and being grateful.

Initially I was afraid to tell others of my diagnosis for fear of what they might think. As I felt better about myself, I began telling a few friends to garner their support and gauge their reactions. Thankfully, most were supportive, but some seemed to withdraw or keep their distance. My main support has always been (and always will be) my husband. Chuck has been my rock from day one and lets me know I am loved and accepted in whatever crazy things I attempt. He just shakes his head, laughs, and encourages me to be me. Chuck and a couple of supportive girlfriends make life easier.

My art also brought me back to the Creator I had somehow lost touch with over time. I've always seen God's handiwork in awesome sunsets, sunrises, and majestic mountains. Now I also look for Him in the faces of people I meet and in the mundane and ordinary things of life. This reconnection has helped me find balance spiritually, emotionally, intellectually, and socially—at least to some degree, socially. I'm still working on that piece.

In early 2015, halfway through this process, I retired from my state position. As I continue my climb out of the valley, I've remained cognizant that it's a daily struggle to stay on the bright side. "One day at a time," is one of my mantras. When I catch myself sliding downhill, I dig in my heels and reach out to a supportive husband and an understanding friend.

This was not how I expected life to be after I retired from the military, but I wouldn't change it. I've learned so much about myself on this journey, and I'll continue to learn more. What I've learned includes trusting myself and others again; *should-a, would-a, could-a* expends too much energy and holds me in the past; anxiety about the future won't change anything but will stress me out; pain has its place and can be dealt with; and fear can be a trap if I let it linger. But, most importantly, I know I am loved, loved by an awesome God, by a wonderful husband, and by family and friends. As long as there is that light, there is hope in my world, and with that hope, a happier, more fulfilling life.

Writing this last piece of my story has been a struggle. There is still such a stigma about depression, PTSD, and mental illness, in general. But if only one person reads this and finds hope and seeks help, then it will be worth putting my story out there.

R Hall
Bosnia 2004

Laura McKee joined the Air Force Reserves prior to Operation Desert Shield in 1990 at twenty-one years old. She has served at Grissom Air Reserve Base in Indiana throughout her twenty-six years of service with assignments in the transportation field, as a jet engine mechanic, and, for the majority of her service, as an in-flight refueler (boom operator). She is a veteran of Desert Storm, Enduring Freedom, Iraq Freedom, Unified Protector, and Inherent Resolve.

ACCOMPLISHING MY MISSION

LAURA McKEE

Uncle Weldon's Flag

I NEVER HEARD HIS VOICE, never felt his touch. Yet Uncle Weldon is one of my true inspirations.

When my cousins and I were young, Uncle Weldon was already gone. He did not relocate because of employment opportunities. He was gone—entirely. He paid the ultimate sacrifice after being drafted to serve during the Korean War. Detailed to working on roads and bridges, he died when a land mine detonated. We never knew if Weldon accidentally set off the bomb or someone else did. He was lost so young and in a world unfamiliar to him.

Our family is close with only a few of us separated by distance. In my younger years I liked to sit at a kitchen table with a glass of milk and listen to my great-uncle talk about the past, including Uncle Weldon. I spent holidays with all of my cousins, aunts, uncles, grandparents, great-aunts, and great-uncles. Our gatherings were at houses on the farms established by my great-great-grandparents. My grandma had five brothers who were smart, funny, loving, and hard working. I knew them all, except for one.

I am still intrigued by Uncle Weldon. He had red hair and, like the rest of his brothers, was tall and lanky. He was the youngest of the siblings, and from what I understand, had a great sense of humor. After high school he did not have a sense of direction. He did not have a plan for his future and hung out with those classmates who also seemed unclear about their life path. Uncle Weldon followed the rules and signed up for the draft. The lottery decided he'd be in the Army.

After finishing Basic Training, Weldon received an assignment to join an engineering battalion. He completed schooling for his trade, and then the Army shipped him to Korea. He sent home pictures of his new friends and of his barracks. Smiling kids often surrounded him—kids he taught how to throw and catch a baseball and how to play kickball. Remembering her brother, my grandma commented many times about how he enjoyed children.

My mother's first cousin now occupies the family farmhouse. The exterior has been re-sided and metal has replaced slate on the roof, but the interior has been only slightly remodeled. My grandmother told me many stories from her past growing up in that same house. Even now I appreciate their way of life and its absence of modern technology. Grandma would sometimes talk about Weldon. Once she mentioned his funeral. When he died, Alaska and Hawaii were not yet states. In fact, Dwight Eisenhower was elected just one month prior to Weldon's death and didn't take office until January of 1953. It wasn't until six years later, in 1959, that Alaska and Hawaii became the forty-ninth and fiftieth states. Hence Weldon's U.S. flag, draped over his casket, had only forty-eight stars.

For years I wanted to see that flag. I had to see it for myself and count the stars. One day I was up in the attic at the farm and went to look for his flag. There it was—folded exactly like the soldiers attending the funeral presented it to Weldon's father. Well, being the curious great-niece of Weldon that I was— and at that point naïve of military funeral traditions—I unfolded and spread the flag to its fullest length on the attic floor. I counted those stars. Grandma spoke the truth: forty-eight stars. I stood there staring at the flag in amazement. U.S. and family history was right in front of me. As soon as that special moment was over, I tried to refold the flag properly. Of course my folds were not even close to the original ones. Fortunately, my curiosity did not upset my grandma and she did not scold me.

Grandma later gave me Weldon's flag and his original obituary she had clipped and saved from the local newspaper. I sometimes wonder what Uncle Weldon would be like if he had survived the war. How many more cousins would we share holiday dinners with? I would love to sit down with my Uncle Weldon over a glass of milk and hear his story.

I am the only family member in my generation who has joined the military. Maybe part of me did so in honor of my great-uncle. When deployed to support my country, I oftentimes remember the ultimate sacrifice made by my Uncle Weldon. It puts my mind and soul at ease to know, if I die in the line of duty, my family will remember and respect me for many years as they have him.

Basic Training / Basic Life Lessons

I WELCOMED THE FACT THAT my Basic Training would take place at Lackland Air Force Base (AFB) in San Antonio, Texas. I had good memories of Texas. As a family, we spent a couple of spring breaks visiting with my aunts in Houston. However, from those visits, I learned a healthy respect for the Texas sun.

One year my sister and I vowed to get the ultimate spring break souvenir: a southern U.S.A. tan. The overcast day impaired our better judgment, and we made a decision to sentence ourselves to an additional thirty minutes in the shackles of the sun. The verdict: my sister's eyes nearly swelled shut and I cringed when the gentlest of humid breezes skimmed my skin. We pretty much put ourselves under house arrest to rehabilitate for the rest of our spring break. Thus, my first step off of the bus in Lackland AFB, a few years later, immediately rendered my respect for the heat, humidity, and sun.

Our welcoming committee at Lackland was a step or more below hospitable. Once we were outside the bus, the training instructors (TIs) screamed at us, called us names, ordered us around, and continuously corrected us. I knew this initiation was coming; after all, I saw the movies *Officer and a Gentlemen* and *Private Benjamin*. I had convinced myself I was prepared, but soon that confidence diminished. Along with accepting harsh verbal treatment, it was important that I follow orders to a T. Everything was to be uniform: clothing, haircuts, and the personal marking of property.

On day two there was a trainee in our flight of thirteen who either ignored a specific order or just did not understand it. We were supposed to simply put our name on the personal property we were allowed to keep (which was very little). When it came to personalizing a bath towel, there were specific rules to follow. The letters had to be an inch tall, in black marker, and at the end of the towel. Well, Airman "K" got an earful after she decorated her towel with a flower shaded in blue, red, and black markers and framed with an artistic border. Oh, we all learned a lesson that day by this one mistake. To get our attention, the TIs made our whole flight do push-ups.

As a flight we did push-ups everywhere for everything at any time. We did push-ups first thing in the morning, during marching drill practice, right before we would run, and just before lights out at night. Each of us also had additional responsibilities, such as cleaning the latrine, scouring the showers, shining boots, dusting lockers, and making our beds. Our TIs encouraged us to discover the talents of each person in our flight. We were to take advantage of those talents and work together for success. It was brought to my attention that I had skills in doing laundry.

I am not sure how those skills were discovered. There was a free laundry facility in our bay, which we shared with other basic trainees, some of whom were weeks ahead of our flight. I learned a lot of valuable information just by listening. I learned how to earn desserts at mealtime, when phone cards could be purchased to call home, that volunteering for weekend extra duty often rendered additional freedom, and that being "recycled" meant your graduation would be delayed and you would be reassigned to another flight. My number one motivator was to avoid being recycled.

Some active duty trainees went into the Air Force not knowing their destination or career. About week five out of six, the Air Force assigned them a technical (tech) school, which led to a job title and a location matching their general test scores. Reservists or trainees in the Air National Guard who enlisted, such as me, were able to choose their careers by vacancies at their unit of choice. All but one career field of my unit of choice had a tech school that followed basic training. I did not want to be away from my family very long so my goal was to complete basic training and return to my assigned base as soon as the military would allow. Since that base was in Indiana—across the street, in fact, from my home—being recycled would have been a huge disappointment.

My best friend and I went into the military on the Buddy System. We were to remain together throughout our training in Basic and OJT. However, after just two weeks of Basic Training, she ended up with a medical emergency that landed her in the hospital and delayed her training for a couple of days. As a result, she did not return to our flight and was recycled. I did not say anything to the TIs for fear of also being recycled for no good reason.

My silence is one of the biggest regrets I have in life, and it taught me a valuable lesson, one of the many life lessons I learned in Basic Training. For instance, I learned if I am ever in a stressful environment, I should remember the big picture and what must be done to accomplish the mission. I learned how to keep a sense of humor and use it appropriately for others and myself. I learned knowledge is power, and, maybe most importantly, I learned not to leave someone behind.

Not speaking up because of fear is my equivalent of leaving someone behind. I am sure my buddy did not want to be recycled, and I could have stopped that procedure by knowing the stipulations of the buddy system and saying something to the leaders of my flight. Luckily, my buddy is forgiving and still remains my friend.

Bahrain

THE CARGO DOOR OPENED AFTER the long flight. I saw darkness in the distance, but the spotlights in our faces obstructed any true view. We were not greeted with the expected desert heat, but rather by a chill, which was borderline cold. The classification "desert" was not keeping its promise of a dry, hot climate.

This was after the Twin Towers had been destroyed and Americans were on the path of revenge. The military was on a full-force mission to search and destroy the enemy and their supporters who had brought forth this act of terror on our own soil. The Air Force placed me and other airmen in the Middle Eastern country of Bahrain to support the United States and other NATO defenses.

Guarded by tanks, the American base in Bahrain was miles away from modern civilization in what seemed to be an unfinished town. Dust, sand, gravel, scorpions, camel spiders, and an ocean of garbage and human waste engulfed us. The only familiarity to home was in the faces of my coworkers.

We resided in a make-shift Tent City, a community which consisted of a narrow main road and rows upon rows of bland tan tents the size of one-car garages. These uniform structures had front entrances equipped with spring-loaded doors, which would slam shut if not controlled. The floors were made of several pallets latched together with plywood on top. Windows were covered with the tents' built-in flaps to keep the outside . . . well, outside. One tent, segregated by gender, housed ten to twelve service members.

We divided our rooms into sections with whatever was left by the residents before us, with whatever we brought, or whatever we found. Sheets, blankets, rugs, and even shower curtains partitioned off our individual living spaces. Inside, there was room for a single cot, a small cabinet, and a single-lane walkway just a bit longer than the cot.

During the hot daylight hours, one generator per tent pumped in cool air. At night each generator shut off when temperatures drastically dropped with the sun. Before leaving home on my adventure, I carefully chose summer clothes because I was going to the desert. I filled my civilian suitcase with shorts, T-shirts, flip-flops, and a bathing suit. I also packed a long-sleeved T-shirt and one pair of long sweatpants. I wore holes in those pants because I wore them so much. We had security guards at the entrance to our Operations buildings. During the nightshift, these guards would bundle up with parkas and gloves. Oftentimes a caring airman would bring them hot chocolate.

We didn't take deployment lightly. We felt that an enemy filled with hatred for our country and with little regard for human life was closer than ever. Prior to every flight we received a briefing of the newest developments pertaining to our mission and surroundings. We carried weapons to the flight line and on every mission. Once we landed we endured debriefings regarding our mission.

There was a consistency in the briefings—the term "Hilltop Haji." It was used to describe an enemy surface to air weapon seen on the move in the mountainous area where we were flying. It was difficult to track or predict this weapon because it was so mobile. It was either carried or pulled by a vehicle that frequently and sporadically relocated it in the rugged terrain. We were in its range of destruction if it were to be fired at us. When flying at night there was little chance we would see it.

We were not the only ones on the lookout, though. The first time we heard of drones actively participating in a conflict was during Operation Enduring Freedom in Afghanistan. Their powerful cameras could see and record action miles away without being noticed. Months went by and Hilltop Haji still posed a threat to our mission; however, we were gaining intel as it was spotted various times by drones flying high in the sky.

One day prior to a flight, we endured our usual routine: we waited for the bus to take us to the other side of the base; we were issued our weapons; we reviewed our mission and procedures; and, finally, we entered the secured room for our secret briefing. We were updated regarding the current changes and then shown a video, a usual practice used to build and sustain our morale. This time our morale-builder was a series of pictures. The first few images were of two shadowy men dressed in dark pants, full turbans, and sandals. They were squatting next to a small, ragged tent, apparently camping on a mountainside. Though the photos appeared to be close-ups taken just a few feet from the site, they were really taken by a drone from at least a mile away. The next series of pictures was shocking. The campsite was destroyed by the same drone that had taken the men's pictures just seconds earlier. At the time, the identity of the two individuals was unknown, but it was certain that they were terrorists. Hilltop Haji was no longer a threat.

If I would rate the places I have served, Bahrain would not be the lowest. It's not a place where I would ever vacation, but I do not wish to bury my experience there, either. Bahrain allows me to appreciate other deployments.

Boots Made for Marching

You carry me to the wild yonder
Staying step-by-step with me in combat
Sustaining my direction
While the rest of me is lost.

You shape yourself by the weight of me
Provide me with comfort as time passes
And we evolve together almost as one.
Some may discard you after time
But I cannot find the heart. Your ruggedness
Supports my occasional exhaustion. Cuts
And blood from battle display our resolution.
The mission is triumphant with us together,
Rather than forfeited when we are apart.

Lisa Wright Wilken enlisted in the United States Air Force in 1993 at the age of twenty-one. She served three years as a medical lab technician working in transfusion services and serving at duty stations in Texas, Nebraska, and Ohio before being medically separated in 1996.

FINDING MY VOICE

LISA WILKEN

Why Did I Enlist?

THAT QUESTION HAUNTS ME. I have been asked it so many times, but I have never been honest, not fully. Truth is, I enlisted in the United States Air Force due to fear. I wish I could say it was to see the world or learn a trade or achieve something noble. But I was simply afraid.

I had an all-American childhood for the most part. The town I grew up in fits every cliché about small towns. You really could miss it if you blinked. Summitville, Indiana, referred to as *Smutville* by the locals, is the highest point between the county seats of two adjoining counties, Madison and Grant. Sports were big in our town. In the spring and summer you played baseball, everybody did, and then there was volleyball and basketball once you got to junior high. Until there was a girls' basketball team, I played on the boys' team, and I was good enough to start. I convinced two other girls to try out with me. I will never forget traveling to other schools and hearing the home team gasp, "They've got girls on their team!" We were the Argylls—no, not socks or sweaters, but fierce Scottish Warriors.

I was the youngest of four children. Being the youngest had some advantages. For instance, I had a special relationship with my father whose nickname for me was Chubby due to my round chipmunk cheeks. My curly hair hung in what my mom called ringlets, but my two sisters called poop curls. The downside to being the youngest was that my sisters never played with me and only tolerated me being around because they had to. My sisters did teach me one thing, though: how to hold my own in a fight. In our neighborhood, unsupervised kids were everywhere since all of our parents worked. Our summer days were filled with outdoor games that sometimes ended in a tussle.

My family life changed dramatically in the early 1980s when one of my siblings died in a car accident. I can still see the kitchen of my childhood home as I walked through the door. The smoke-filled room fell silent. I knew something was wrong. My cousin had come to pick me up from my end-of-season basketball party, but she wouldn't tell me why. When we rounded the curve to our house, I saw cars parked everywhere and wondered if someone had died.

I thought it was my brother. Jim has grown into a wonderful man, but when he was younger he really put some stress on my parents. My first memory of my Bubby is of him sitting slumped at the kitchen table trying very hard to make my parents believe that he and his friends had stumbled upon a case of beer. It was already cold because they found it in a snowdrift.

It wasn't Jim who had died.

A neighbor, the town gossip, stepped between my Aunt Shirley and me and blurted, "Cindy is dead." Cindy was eighteen. It was two days before her senior prom. She and her boyfriend, Rick, along with his two brothers were on their way to pick up the tux when a train hit their car. Cindy died instantly and one brother died later at the hospital. Rick and his other brother survived.

I went with Carolyn, my other sister, to the hospital. I had to go. Everything was in a fog and in slow motion. Only seeing Rick would make it real.

As soon we walked in, Rick said, "I swear I didn't see that train."

Eighteen people lost their lives at that rural crossing before lights and a crossbar were finally erected in the late 1980s. It took a lawsuit by my parents and Rick's parents to initiate that change.

Life for my family was difficult for a long time after that. My parents did what I can't imagine ever having to do—bury a child. When they bought Cindy's plot, they bought ones for themselves, too, and for each of their children. The cemetery caretaker explained how Jim, Carolyn, and I would all grow up and be buried with our family. I felt everyone in our town looked at our family differently after my sister died.

My high school wasn't a lot different than other rural Indiana schools. Some students drove tractors to school. They participated in sports right after school and then headed into the fields, either working for their dad or a buddy's dad. Every kid I knew had a job of some sort: detasseling corn, baling hay, or cleaning the cemetery grounds.

Although we had a wonderful childhood, my siblings and I knew that money didn't grow on trees. Mom worked in a tool and die factory. She came home daily with cuts and abrasions but never complained. Dad worked second shift so he was in bed when we left for school and gone before we got home. When he'd get in from work, we would be asleep. On Fridays he worked a double shift, and on Sunday nights he'd go in for startup around six.

I graduated from high school with a clear path to college, but my financial aid would have included student loans. I went two years, all the while struggling with work and classes. My options seemed exhausted when one of my high school friends suggested we enlist in the Air Force on the "buddy system." *Yeah right,* the military. That is what I thought, but her dad explained the process to us, "how we could write our own ticket." We could see the world and maybe find a career.

My friend was already married and divorced, with no college. At least I had a couple of years, I thought, but that meant nothing and I knew it. I checked out the so-called buddy system and learned that it was real. I also learned that I could get a guaranteed job skill. Without telling anyone, I met with a recruiter. Not until after I signed my paperwork did I tell anyone. I was afraid I would change my mind—chicken out.

Angie chickened out, but I was more afraid of not going, scared I might end up a single mom in my small town, working in a factory and just getting by enough to raise the children I had with my unfaithful high school sweetheart. I would always just be that *little Wright girl*. Maybe I was afraid that my college-educated boyfriend was right: I wasn't worldly. What I did know was that the little Wright girl from Smutville would never let fear stop her.

The last thing my dad said to me before I left for Basic Training struck a new fear in my heart: "Don't come home with anything less than an honorable discharge."

Learning the Rules

THE BUS RIDE FROM THE San Antonio airport to Basic Training was so quiet I could hear the road and the thump of a bad tire. I could even hear my heartbeat. I wanted to talk to the girl next to me just to keep from hearing the questions running through my head: "What have I done?" "Why did I do this?" "Holy Shit, is this real?" I closed my eyes so tight it hurt and silently screamed, "You can do this!" I knew I had no choice.

After the bus arrived, we stood waiting under the overhang of a dorm. Everything was dark except a corner light. Finally, we heard the approach of our Training Instructor (TI)—the click of boot heels. As the clicking got closer, my heart raced faster. I knew not to put my bags down. My recruiter had prepared me well. I knew my reporting statement and how important it was to not get noticed and NEVER volunteer for anything.

There were those who didn't have a recruiter that cared. They not only put down their bags, they sat on them. Turns out, sitting on your bag at Lackland Air Force Base can cause an E-5 to scream. I had never heard a grown man insult and berate someone that long without using any profanity. I was impressed.

Then there was the kid from New Jersey who just couldn't get his reporting statement right. He was third in line. After everyone repeated his statement with him five times, the rest of the line went pretty quick. The New Jersey kid was nicknamed "Water Head" for the rest of Basic.

Our four TIs had big wide hats and attitudes to match. One thing we were told right up front was that our TIs were not allowed to curse us or put their hands on us. It is amazing what other techniques can be used to cut someone down. Who knew being called a flower petal would be a cut down, but anything that meant soft, frail, or weak worked. I am not a flower petal.

There were enough women to form an all-female flight. Our flight had two male TIs, so that first night a female TI took us to our dorm and issued our flight jackets and paperwork. She missed the briefing on not cursing us and lovingly referred to us as "fucking nasty ass females" as she explained that we could not flush tampons down a urinal. We were assigned beds and told that reveille would be at 5 a.m. It was currently 3:45 a.m. As I climbed into bed, I could hear whimpers from some in the bay as they tried to be quiet. Again, my heart raced, and I yelled in my head, "What the HELL did you do?" I took a deep breath or two and heard that calm voice respond, "You can do this."

Morning came and the TIs began screaming. Their screams lasted for several days. My recruiter had told me that they would make an example of everything so others would learn. Good idea. Yeah, until you are the one walking around the outside of the building, clicking your dog tags together saying, "Moo, moo, I'm a cow." This was because my dog tags were outside my shirt.

Another rule was that your rubber hair band had to match your hair color. There was one girl who came to basic training with blue hair. She got sent to get it fixed, but I don't remember her name because after that she was always called *Blue*. The names you were given stuck. I was *Olive Oil*. We had a *Mouse, Cricket,* and *Bambi*. I think back on it now and laugh. I bet those TIs had fun at parties telling stories about us. I wonder how many times they put someone in a locker to play Juke Box. Each time the TI dropped a coin through the vent, you had to sing a song.

Our two TIs had distinctive personalities. The staff sergeant was about 5'8" tall, and we referred to him as *Dad*. The other, a sergeant from Bolivia, was over six feet, and he was our evil *Step-Dad*. He scared me enough so that I never ate dessert because I would have had to walk in front of the "snake pit"—the table where he and the other TIs sat to eat.

Since my dorm chief was on a weight program, I didn't have many opportunities to turn down dessert anyway. The rule was that when your dorm chief is done eating, you are done eating. When she stands up, you swallow what is in your mouth and stand up. Since my last name started with a W, I was at the end of the line. She was right behind me. We were required to drink two glasses of water at every meal, so I had just enough time to sit down, swallow my water, and cram whatever I could into my mouth before the dorm chief drank her water, took one bite, and stood back up.

I weighed 128 at the beginning of Basic and 114 at the end. When my mom hugged me after graduation, she pushed me back and squeezed me. She said, "You are hard all over." I felt strong. I was strong.

Our dorm had two bays that each held twenty-five women. In the Day Room there was furniture, but we weren't allowed to sit on it. We never earned the privilege since Air Force Basic Training is only six weeks long. I can say *only* now, but at the time, it seemed to go on and on. And all that time we sat on the floor and never once on the furniture—even when our TIs weren't there.

The dorm's Orderly Room would communicate with us through a speaker box. One night one of the girls in my flight jokingly popped to attention in front of the speaker box and said, "Scottie, Scottie, beam me up." We all laughed. Then we heard a voice say, "Why don't you beam your little ass down here?" They had no idea who she was, but she did just that. She got dressed and went down and then had KP (Kitchen Patrol) the next two days.

Everyone in Basic Training goes to church. Church is a break. You don't get yelled at, and they are nice to you. It is joyful. I went to church every Sunday, and I cried every time.

I was lucky that my recruiter had let me know what to expect. I knew Basic was a game to teach us to work together, to believe in ourselves and a greater cause. I knew about the confidence course and history of the Air Force, but I don't think anyone can really prepare you fully.

They can't tell you about the people who will be in your flight. For six weeks there was a woman in front of me in line whose name was Wong. Mine was Wright. She was just tall enough to be in the military, and I am 5'8". The joke: "I wonder if two Wongs make a Wright?" It never seemed to get old. We did a lot of running for our TIs because they liked to yell, "Hey Wright and Wong get over here!"

There was the rough girl from Philly who got caught with a pencil in her pants that she was using as an eyeliner and the seventeen-year-old who had to convince her parents to sign to let her go. Yoman was a skinny girl from D.C. who had the biggest feet I had ever seen. With her boots on, she had clown feet. She had a clown's spirit, too; she wanted to make people laugh. At night between the TV theme songs we sang, she entertained us with her antics. We all had such different backgrounds, but these theme songs were something we all knew. Our favorites were the themes to *Brady Bunch* and *Addams Family*.

Every morning, some designated person woke us up one minute before the TIs came in screaming. We slept in our shirts, bras, underwear, socks, and blousing straps. That way we could pull on our pants, step into our boots, and slip on our jacket as we walked down three flights of stairs. That is how much time you had to get buttoned and your hat on before you hit the door where someone was waiting. It became routine. We did it like robots. I can still hear the safety patrol: "Walk, don't run. Use the handrails. Think safety." We re-peated this chant as we descended the stairs and stepped through the funky morning breath of all those before us. The bright light of the stairwell blinded us, and we were so tired we could feel the bags under our eyes. At the doorway, our hats went on and our eyes met the darkness outside. We sang the Air Force song every morning in the dark.

We were an Honor Flight. Other than bragging rights, it got us to the front of the chow line. Our brother Flight didn't do so well. Our TI told us early on that if we wanted to kick their cans we would have to do it early. He told us that when the men shave their heads, they lose all their common sense. But, if we start out well, by the time they get it together, we will be untouchable. He was right. Our brother Flight could not run, march, or even line up right for about two weeks.

Later in Basic, I was "promoted" to Latrine Queen. This is not what they called me, though. It was the rule of the Latrine Bitch that we would use only the first two toilets and all fifty-two of us could shower in three minutes. We had a system. You got wet at the first shower, soaped and shampooed at the next, and by the time you reached the last showerhead, you better be rinsed because you were done.

I used my position to make a deal with the dorm chief: if she would let me eat on Friday and Saturday nights then we would take long showers on those nights. However, no bribe could have enticed me to allow anyone to comb or brush her hair in the latrine. That was to be done in a personal area, just like boot polishing. That way, if you didn't clean up properly, it was on you and only you.

Each night I was woken up for an inspection of the Latrine. The TIs would turn the light off and shine a flashlight on the tile floor to look for dust. Most nights, they didn't find much. We had learned to spray our T-shirts with starch and use them to wipe the floor. Before putting those T-shirts in our laundry bags, we had to remember to turn them right side out. I learned that a drop of baby oil rubbed on my hands before running them down the stainless steel shelf along the mirror helped hide the dust that settled there. It seemed as if they pumped the dust in while we slept.

By the time I left Basic Training, I was an airman. I didn't know it, but I would never be a civilian again.

Technical School at Sheppard AFB

AFTER BASIC, I WENT STRAIGHT to my Technical School at Sheppard AFB in Wichita Falls, Texas. I felt strong after boot camp and ready to learn the skills of a laboratory technician.

School was both interesting and challenging. We went through an entire year of chemistry in about six weeks. This intense schooling helped us to quickly become a cohesive unit; we were always together studying or in class. We also lived and ate together. By the way, it's true what they say about the Air Force taking care of their own. Our dining facility had awesome food, and our rooms were nice with study desks, plenty of storage, a mini fridge, and a private bathroom with a shower. Although our dorms were co¬ed, each floor was same sex.

In Technical School we earned privileges back from Basic Training where they told us when and how to do everything and screamed at any failure until everyone fell into line. Four phases at Technical School led to ever-increasing freedom. During Phase I, we had to be in uniform at all times, abstain from alcohol even if we were twenty-one, and submit to a ten o'clock curfew. I believe that curfew saved many people from making stupid mistakes when they were unleashed from Basic Training. In Phase II, we could take our uniform off after duty hours, stay out until midnight on weekends, and drink if we were at least twenty-one. By Phase III, there was no weekend curfew and we could wear civilian clothing during duty hours if not on duty. Finally, in Phase IV, we could drive during duty hours to and from class.

Every morning we had formation and our school schedule was determined by our shift. I was B Shift. I went to school from noon until 6 p.m. During our mandatory study period from 6-8 a.m., we had to be in uniform and ready for inspection—at our desk studying with the door open. I only remember officers coming to check twice in three months, but when they did come, someone would suffer. The punishment for sleeping at your desk was an unexpected and unpleasant screaming alarm; if you forgot to lock your locker or left your locker keys on your bed, then the punishment for that would be much worse—a trashed room. They would throw everything from your drawers and flip your bed. Clean-up was bad enough, but then you also had to live with an angry roommate. I took precautions; my keys hung on a chain around my neck.

We were free to go to Physical Training (PT) after 8 a.m., but we had to be in formation at 11:45. As graduation approached, my Flight, like the others, would shout out how many "wake ups" we had left. Attending Technical School was somewhat like going to college, only with a big brother watching.

Tech School prepares you for a profession. It awakens the new you: the confident new Airman who makes the cut every week in his or her field to advance. If you "wash out" in Basic, you are recycled back to re-learn your "issue," but in Tech school, if you wash out, you become whatever is needed—supply clerk, cook, or security police. I busted my ass studying so I wouldn't fail. Chemistry was hard for me, but, because I buckled down and struggled with it, I developed good study habits. They helped me excel throughout Tech School.

We took time to have fun. I danced, drank, and played pool and softball (badly). We connected as young adults facing an unknown future. What we didn't have on base, we could find right outside the gate. I visited Dallas and also Waco, just after it became infamous. Oklahoma City was only two hours away. I had a great time, and now have wonderful memories of people who would never have been in my life if I hadn't taken that oath.

A Turn for the Worse

FOR MY ON-THE-JOB TRAINING (OJT), I put down on my "dream sheet" that I wanted to go anywhere on the East or West Coasts or to Florida or Texas. I was sent to Offutt, AFB in Omaha, Nebraska. Despite my disappointment, I learned that Nebraska is beautiful and Omaha has a lot to offer.

In OJT, I attended school three days a week for two hours and spent the rest of my workdays in the lab under the rotating supervision of staff. In a short amount of time, the USAF taught me to work in chemistry, hematology, serology, microbiology, blood banking, virology, and urinalysis. I learned to draw blood—for testing and donating. We practiced on each other, which meant we needed trust and luck. Eventually, we became excellent "sticks"—for the most part, but there was one student in each class you never wanted to be paired with. If you were, you just accepted the fact that you'd have to resist making a noise and that later you'd have bruises.

Offutt is where my experience in the military took a sharp turn, which jolted me so hard I didn't see the wall I slammed into.

I was raped. I still have trouble saying that. Rape is a crime that assaults a person's soul but leaves no visible mark. You are left with a burning empty space that is never filled and tries to spoil everything you love or enjoy. I remember the events of that time period as if they happened yesterday. I can feel them; I smell them as if I haven't washed. There's a feeling of *nothing*. Feeling like *nothing* is what I remember most.

The emergency room doctor was kind as he examined me, took pictures, and collected samples. He treated me with antibiotics for any possible transmission of disease, tested me for HIV and pregnancy, and gave me his version of today's FDA-approved morning-after pill. The lights seemed brighter than usual as I watched what was happening as if in a movie I was in.

I was released to two male officers of Special Investigations who took me from the hospital. It was a long ride to their office, which seemed to happen in slow motion. I could hear my heart beating and a distracting "white" noise in my head. For hours I answered these officers' questions while I was being recorded and watched behind a two-way mirror. Now that I look back, as mad as I am at myself for the final outcome of my case, I realize I didn't do too badly answering their questions. I didn't do too badly through the entire process . . . until at the end. But there is no end.

That OSI interview was grueling. I answered questions, gave any detail they wanted, and described my entire sexual history from the time I lost my virginity to the night I was raped. I felt like a robot spitting out information. I was wearing my uniform and thought I had to answer every question I was asked. The military has no rape shield law. I felt like government property.

My roommate and I had gone out to dinner that night. When we came home, we read John Grisham books in our beds and talked to our moms on the phone. At nine o'clock we went to a going-away party in the dayroom, returning after 1:00 a.m. when the dayroom closed. We continued to hang out in the room across the hall, and, when the party ended, I went to my room, removed my makeup, put on my nightshirt and went to bed. My roommate packed a bag and went to her boyfriend's. I fell asleep.

I awoke to pressure on my chest and warmth between my legs. With blacked out windows, it was pitch black in our room. As soon as I realized what was happening, I threw my right arm up and hit something with my forearm. The pressure on my chest lifted somewhat, but my left arm was pinned under me. In seemingly one swift motion, my body pushed out from underneath him and tumbled onto the floor. I lunged for the light. That light was almost blinding, but in it I saw him and his red underwear as he ran out. Apparently I had made a lot of noise getting loose from his grip because the guy across the hall came to the door.

After the OSI interview, I was taken back to the hospital. Our acting first sergeant let me call home on his office phone. Those two phone calls were harder than having the two OSI officers ask if I felt any pleasure while being assaulted. My mom told me to find someone to talk to. I don't remember much about the call to my boyfriend (now my husband).

My acting first shirt took me to the mental health building and dropped me off in front. That night I met with a civilian social worker who helped me process what had happened and helped prepare me for what would be coming as best she could. After that, I was dropped off in front of my dormitory. It was December, and I had no coat on as I stood frozen for a few minutes afraid to go in, but not sure why. I knew who assaulted me, and I knew they said they were picking him up. I finally made it up the three flights of stairs and down the long hallway to the second to last room on the right. Once inside, I locked my door as fast as I could. Not just the automatic but also the deadbolt lock. I moved a chair in front of the door as if it could do something if the lock and deadbolt failed.

Uncontrollable fear scared me the most. I waited. It will get better. It didn't. *Okay,* I thought, *I will go ahead and take the medicine. It will help.* It made it feel like I didn't have anything to deal with. I floated. I cried. I hid. I didn't know yet that you can't hide. Fear will always find you.

What Followed

THE INVESTIGATION AND ARTICLE 32 hearing process is somewhat of a blur to me, though discussions and dreams will trigger vivid memories. Because of the assault, I felt like a sticky blank canvas—so sticky that situations stuck and their implications caused problems. Throughout the investigation I was told how strong I was, but I felt weak. The experience itself and the belief that justice was futile tested my physical and emotional limits.

They tell you the drugs are there to help. Because I took an antidepressant, a mood stabilizer, an antipsychotic for anxiety, and something to help me sleep, I didn't feel anything for a while. Eventually your body becomes used to the drugs, but your mind doesn't get used to the trauma of your body being violated.

One OSI officers asked, "Since you weren't aware of the entire assault, does that make it easier?" I wish.

Between the investigation and the wait for the Article 32 hearing, my four pills a day helped, but there was no way I could sleep. Vodka and orange juice mixed with Klonopin helped in that department—at least at first. When I started swallowing half and then filling the glass back up with vodka, I knew I was in trouble.

By then I was living in NCO quarters. One evening I told a perfect stranger why I was there and he listened. He told me he had seen me come and go and knew something must be wrong but didn't want to pry. That night, sitting in the dayroom, I was too afraid to go into my room. I was afraid of myself. If this man hadn't started a conversation, I would have gone in that room and taken all of my sleeping pills and mood stabilizers. I would have drunk my nightly drink and hoped to not wake up. But when he asked if I was okay, I couldn't hold back. *Thank you, Scott. You saved my life.*

If not for my First Sergeant, I might have still been staying alone in my old dorm room. He had me moved to a new dorm when he learned that I was still in the same room and that my assaulter had tried to contact me. My roommate had moved out before I came back from emergency leave because she didn't want to be associated with a rape trial. She later apologized and told me she felt guilty for leaving me alone that night; she had seen my attacker enter our hall as she was leaving, though she had no idea what he was headed to do. I understood and accepted her apology.

After I moved to that new dorm, my attacker had his friend give me a message. I lived in fear. In the military, unless you are a flight risk or accused of a capital crime, you are not incarcerated until convicted. He had been charged and released.

Because I would see my attacker in the dining hall, I ate vending machine food. I'd also see him in the lab. I was moved from my job, and since I wasn't allowed to talk about my rape, people had the impression I'd done something wrong. After I was moved to the base hotel (where I had to pay for my room), they found me a spot in NCO quarters on the other side of the base. I was the only female in that building, and I was only twenty-two years old. I got attention that I didn't want, but I kept to myself and my newness and gender finally faded in.

My First Sergeant stepped in again when he found out that our Command was planning to give my attacker an Article 15 which is a non-judicial punishment. He called our Commander and told him not to accept that agreement and that he needed to hear from me. I was shocked that a non-judicial punishment could even be considered. The First Sergeant took me to meet with the Commander. After I described what had occurred, my Commander immediately called the Chief Military Justice and said "no" to the Article 15.

The next step was filing an Article 32, a proceeding under the Uniform Code of Military Justice, which is similar to a Grand Jury in civilian court. My attacker was charged with breaking in, rape, and sodomy. He was charged with one attempted count on each charge as well. In case they couldn't prove that he completed the acts, the attempt charges carried the same punishment.

The assault happened in December and charges were referred in April. I did nothing except survive during those months. Some days my First Sergeant would have me help out in the pharmacy or in the orderly room, but my OJT stopped. Once the charges came through, though, I could leave to finish my training. I was moved to Wright Patterson in Dayton, Ohio, to be closer to home. I graduated from OJT as a lab technician and took the National Registry test while on Active Duty to become registered with the American Society of Clinical Pathologists. I was named Student of the Quarter and was nominated for Senior Airman Below the Zone.

Life was moving forward, but I wasn't. I was still scared, but *why?* I was so angry, but at *who?* I needed help. What do I say? People told me I was strong and brave while I beat myself up for living a lie. *If they only knew how weak I felt. . . .*

When it was time for the Court Martial, the special prosecutor brought me back to Offutt. We met two days in a row going over my testimony. He asked me everything and showed me what it would be like on the stand by taking the role of defense. The OSI investigation was grueling. Recounting the night in the Article 32 was hard, but it was nothing compared to being the star witness in a rape trial. I was 22 years old and alone. The DOD had not yet developed the Sexual Assault Response Team (SART), and civilian advocates were not allowed on base.

After our last mock session, I went back to my hotel to try and rest before the big day, but I was called back later that night. The special prosecutor and Chief Military Justice explained that the defense had made a motion to accept an Other Than Honorable Discharge in lieu of Court Martial, but they would do it only if I agreed. I asked the prosecutor what he thought. I was young and naïve enough to feel like they were my lawyers.

"Lisa, I can prove he raped you, but the rape wasn't violent enough for him to get any real jail time."

I knew what he was telling me. He had just put me through hell—and my going through it again in public wasn't going to give me what I was looking for—for it to be over. I was young, alone, and I agreed. I thought my hell would be over. It wasn't. They did have him processed and off the base in three days. I was assured it would be on his records. I then found out that he had attempted to do the same thing at his previous base, but a roommate came in and stopped it. I have never had the courage to look to see if he has harmed another woman.

Before heading back to my permanent duty station, I was called in. My former Commander explained that no other case would be handled like mine. They didn't take pictures of the dorm room that I was raped in—they were relying on sketches. They had no pictures of my torn underwear found at the foot of the bed, and they didn't keep them. They didn't keep the chewing gum that had to be cut out of my pubic hair.

I think the Commander realized that the fact that they were not prepared to deal with such a crime had added to the injuries I was dealt. I credit my First Sergeant for making him understand. My First Sergeant had a loved one who was a rape survivor. That survivor helped me without ever meeting me—by using her voice.

Going on with your life after something like rape isn't easy, but you do the best you can and I did. Unfortunately, I had to have two surgeries after the assault because the lining of my uterus was now on the outside of my uterus. I had endometriosis, migraines, and PTSD from Military Sexual Trauma (MST). I have always said that MST is the DOD and VA's cowardly way of categorizing rape survivors of friendly fire.

I served three-and-a-half years in the military. My experiences, like those of others, include the good and the bad. I had the worst experience of my life during my service, but as much as I hate it, it is part of who I am. It has shaped me into the woman I am today and impacted the woman I want to be. I choose to use my PTSD for good and not evil. After the military, I have continued to serve by volunteering with Veteran Service Organizations, using my experiences to help others in similar situations. I speak up about my experience, not only to help others know they don't have to suffer in silence, but because I can't be silent.

I am proud of my service now, but only because someone helped me find my voice. In 2012 I met the State Women Veteran Coordinator for Indiana, Ashley Roberts, who connected with me on a level I didn't even understand. She could see me; she could see my struggle. I didn't have to hide. I couldn't hide. Before then, I wasn't proud of my service. I was ashamed because that's how my experiences made me feel.

I know that the military didn't set out to harm me. I also know that the USAF didn't set out to re-victimize me by not having a good system set up to handle this issue. I also know that none of that matters today. The past is what it is, and I choose how to handle it from here on out. In 2012 I first let others hear my veteran voice. I spoke the word *rape* out loud, in my own voice. It was a moving experience to open myself up and be so vulnerable in a room full of strangers—but were they strangers? By the time I finished speaking at the 2012 Hoosier Women Veterans Conference, I felt such relief. As I spoke, I saw the nods of women who knew exactly what I was talking about. They had lived through something similar, knew someone who had, or sympathized with me. I saw tears wiped away when I spoke about how people I knew and thought highly of avoided me because they didn't want to be associated with a rape trial. Some of those tears were for me, and some might have sprung from guilt—from what they themselves had done in an attempt to survive.

The best part of speaking up was that it allowed me to start letting go. Iron-ically, letting go meant acknowledging that my assault will never be over: it is part of me. I also started to learn that forgiveness, forgetting, and letting go are all different things and they are needed for different reasons.

There were women waiting to speak to me after the conference. I heard stories that had never been shared before. Since then, I have testified before Congress, fulfilling a promise I made in 1994. When my Commander assured me that no other case would be handled like mine in the future, I told him to write my name down because he would hear it again. I knew what I could say while I wore the uniform, but I wouldn't wear it forever.

In my congressional testimony in 2013, I started with this introduction: *"Hello, my name is Lisa Wilken. I am a USAF Veteran and I want to talk to you about one voice and what it can do. Some of us never find our voice and others run from our voice afraid that if we listen to it, we will act foolishly or on emotion. As women, we are always guarded in that way. Here is my story of me finding my voice and the courage to use it."*

I have a wonderful life with my husband of twenty years. He's an under-standing man with the patience of a saint. We have been blessed with two beautiful boys, ten years apart in age. They are the best of each of us, but more like my husband than me.

I want to emphasize one point I have always tried to make clear: Not every man in the military is a rapist. There are a small number of predators, but they sometimes have a long career of hurting others. Men and women in the military, who wear the uniform honorably, do not want this happening to our brothers and sisters. Yes, I said *brothers*. Their silent suffering is just as real, if not worse.

The Rest of the Story

THERE IS A PORTION OF my story that I have never told publicly because I've wanted to retain some dignity. By staying silent, I've let this part of the story hold me in its tight grip.

Let's go back to the point in which the special prosecutor said, "Lisa, I can prove that he raped you, but the rape wasn't violent enough for him to get any real jail time." That's where I normally end that portion of the story. But there's more to it. Without taking a breath, he went on to say, "And if there is one Right to Life member on the jury, they'll see you as a murderer and therefore got what you deserved."

I was angry at the first statement. I thought to myself, *if he had beat my ass, would they do something then?* But my response to the second statement was worse than shock. I was crushed. You have to remember that you have no privacy when you are in the military. My medical records were accessible to the defense. That was something else the E.R. doctor forgot to tell me—along with how sick his version of the morning-after pill would make me. He also neglected to mention what would have to happen if that drug cocktail didn't prevent the rape from resulting in pregnancy. Those who should have stood by me took something that is the most grueling and hardest decision that any woman ever makes and used it against me. I have always felt I was blackmailed into staying quiet. Because of my silence, a repeat offender was free to repeat his offense.

I had taken my mom back out with me to Omaha, Nebraska, so that I wouldn't be alone when I testified. I hadn't told my mom about my earlier decision. That was something that I didn't ever want to tell her. That is why I agreed to let the U.S. Air Force give the man who raped me an Other Than Honorable Discharge. What's so ironic is that I went straight back to the hotel that night and told my mom everything.

When I was assured at Offutt that no other case would be handled the way mine was, I said, "Write my name down because you will hear it again." Now you know why.

The Other Side of Service

AFTER I WAS MEDICALLY SEPARATED from the Air Force, I went on with my life. I did what most young people do, I got a job, and I got married. I tried to pretend as though my time in the service didn't actually happen. I didn't talk about it with friends or family or coworkers. It was as though those years didn't happen. Boy was I really living a lie.

And that lie ended when I had an unnecessary surgery at a VA Medical Center. They told me a pregnancy test was positive, that I was having my second miscarriage in a year, and that I needed a D&C. There were complications after the surgery, and my bowels stopped working. The on-call doctor didn't realize that I had been a lab technician in the military and could understand all of her "doctor-speak" as she was reading my chart and thinking out loud. A beta HCG, which tells how pregnant you are, had been done during surgery and was negative—but there's no way a Qualitative HCG, which tells you yes or no, could be positive and then a Beta HGC done a few hours later, in surgery, could be negative. I realized that the test had been reported incorrectly. I hadn't been pregnant, wasn't having a miscarriage, and had had the D&C because someone had made a mistake.

Things got better as we were able to work through my medical issues and my bowels began moving. I asked to see all of my lab work, and the women's health program manager said she would get them for me. When I hadn't heard from her by 4 p.m. that afternoon, I called and she told me the truth. The original pregnancy test was never completed; it was still pending in the hospital lab computer. The hospital administration had been made aware of the situation and someone would be contacting me.

A few days later I received a phone call from The VA Medical Center Director; the Chief of Ambulatory Care and the Women's Coordinator were also on the line. They explained that their root cause analysis showed human error. When the nurse looked into the computer, she knew the name of the test she was looking for, but didn't pay attention to the date. She reported a lab result that was nine months old, from a miscarriage I'd had earlier that year. The mistake sent me to surgery.

I naively asked, "What mechanism are you going to put into your system so that this error can't happen in the future?" The answer was, "There will not be any changes in Indianapolis unless they are done nationally and that will not be something that is done."

It was at that exact moment, sitting at my dining room table having that conference call, that every victim feeling that I had had and worked through or told myself that I had worked through hit me like a ton of bricks. I could barely contain my anger. Again something had happened to me at the hands of the government and nothing would be done about it. What I heard in my mind was, "You are nothing."

The women's coordinator, Laura, was a wonderful lady, and she heard the change in the tone of my voice. She asked, "Lisa, do I need to get you somebody to talk to?" And she was so right because I needed someone. Laura Malone set me up with a person at the Vet Center because I had told her I wouldn't come back to the hospital. I started seeing a therapist twice a week.

During that time I was contacted by the VA Medical Center Director to talk about making this "right." During one conversation I explained to him that I had never had to handle anything like this before and said I thought I might need to get someone to speak for me. He offered me $15,000 to not get an attorney involved. This made me feel so dirty that I told him I wouldn't accept any more calls from him. I knew that the VA's tactics weren't directed at me. But what had happened was so very personal to me—again. This time I knew I was not going to stay silent; I was going to speak out and stand up for myself. And I did. I got an attorney and sued the United States of America for medical malpractice.

Suing the United States of America is complicated. First, you have to give them notice that you're going to sue them and why. Then they have a hundred and eighty days to respond. Once they respond, you can officially file in court. But during those one hundred and eighty days negotiations happen. First, the VA claimed that the doctor who performed the surgery was not a VA employee and therefore I should sue him directly. I had no fault with him. He took great care of me given the information that he received from the VA employee.

Next, the VA made the argument that I was already considered a disabled veteran prior to the surgery and I couldn't sue them because of that. I was offered a lump sum for the unnecessary surgery with an offset—which meant that I'd get the lump sum, but they'd take away an equal amount of my service connected disability compensation for post traumatic stress, endometriosis, depression, and migraines. The government shouldn't have to pay twice for the same injury, the U.S. Attorney's office said. They cited some cases that sounded legitimate. But in my mind I kept saying . . . "Hey wait a minute. This is for the negligence of the surgery and that is for disabilities I received while in service."

Thank God for the Internet. I put my information about the unnecessary surgery and the settlement talks on a forum online, and I got a private message explaining when offsets are and aren't applicable. They were not applicable in my case because it was clearly stated that you couldn't use service-connected disability pay to offset a court settlement or judgment.

My attorney didn't want to listen to me, so in our last settlement conference with the Federal Magistrate, I asked to speak. I provided the U.S. Attorney, the Magistrate, and my attorney a copy of the VA's regulations about offsets and said, "I believe the VA through the U.S. Attorney's office has tried to perpetrate a fraud upon the court by offering a settlement they legally could not make. I went into the VA Medical Center for treatment for a service-connected disability and incurred medical negligence, and, as a result, I am eligible to sue the United States under the Federal Tort Claims Act."

The Magistrate thanked me and asked me and my attorney to wait outside for a few minutes. When we returned, the U.S. Attorney was no longer present and we were informed that our settlement conference would continue at a later date, when the U.S. Attorney's office could come to the table with a legitimate settlement offer. Eventually, I settled the medical malpractice suit for much less than what I could have received if I'd taken it to court, but it was never about the money for me. It was about standing up for myself and making a difference and making a change for others in the future.

While I was going through all this, I wrote a proposal for how the VA could fix their Computerized Patient Record System (CPRS) so that what happened to me couldn't happen to another veteran. It involved creating a safety step that would allow only current admission or current pending tests to come up when a patient's social security number is typed into the program.

Trying to get VA officials to listen to me was impossible, so I reached out to my congressman. When that didn't work, I tried my senators. One senator's office sent me a huge packet, which, to my shock, held personal information about another veteran who had contacted the office for help: Social Security numbers, addresses, bank information, inventory records. At that point I hadn't spoken publicly about my experiences and I was terrified that some strange person might have gotten a packet with all of my personal information. The senator's office was very apologetic, but I knew they weren't really paying attention to the issue.

I never did get a response from the other senator's office. I followed up with their office on a regular basis to check to see if they had gotten a response from the VA and was told repeatedly that as soon as they got something they'd let me know. Finally, after six months I was told to stop calling. There I sat at my kitchen table, fighting back the feeling of being useless and nothing and trying to crawl out of depression. Then I looked at my computer and saw the office of the Senate Chaplain on the screen. So I called there. I got lucky because the Senate Chaplain's Chief of Staff answered the phone and listened to my story. He told me to send him the information I had sent my senator and he would give it to the senator's Chief of Staff. That same afternoon, the person who had told me not to call again called to set a phone appointment with the senator for the next day.

But when something actually happened it was because a Congresswoman overheard some staffers on the Veteran's Committee talking about a Hoosier veteran and the Indianapolis VA Medical Center and she sent her staff to get the information. Her Chief of Staff called and asked me to send them the package I'd sent to my senators. He put me on the safe list, which meant the package wouldn't be delayed by security screenings. Less than forty-five days later, I received a letter from the Department of Veterans Affairs. They had found my computer proposal to have Merit, and it had been assigned a National Service Request Number. My suggested changes went live in every VA medical center on January 1st, 2011.

That experience made me realize that we need to know our legislators and have our legislators know us. It made me realize that one voice can make a difference, and that I am not nothing. My service matters, I matter. Today I believe it's not a weakness to tell someone that you're having a hard time. I suffered in silence for many years, keeping my pain to myself, but I did harm to myself in doing that. If I can help others to not make the same mistakes that I've made, I've done something good and that helps me. I choose that, and I choose to let my bad experiences motivate me to make positive things happen.

I truly believe that my experience in the military has shaped me into the woman that I am today. We all have things we carry with us, and it is what we choose to do with those things that makes us into the people we are. I am a wife, a mother, and a veteran.

The Lighthearted Side of My Service

NOW AFTER FINDING MY VOICE and not being ashamed of my service, I can look back and re-live the good parts. I realize that Basic Training was a blast and I'd do it again in a heartbeat just to get back into physical shape. I was the strongest I've ever been in my life. I also had a great time in technical school, doing what young people do—going out dancing and hanging out with young people of diverse backgrounds from all over the United States. I remember the pride I felt marching in my first parade. It was sunny and hot and my dress blues were itchy, my shoes excruciatingly painful, but I could not have stood any straighter or more proudly. What follows are a few favorite memories from my service.

* * *

When we would get newbies in the laboratory, we'd play jokes on them—like send them down to the supply room to get fallopian tubes. We would show them a capillary crit tube, and they would eagerly run down to the supply room to retrieve some. When they came back, the look on their face was absolutely precious. The best part was watching how they waited to pull the same prank on the next newbie. Going down for fallopian tubes became a rite of passage.

* * *

At one point I moved off base and lived with three other women. One of these women was from California. She had the confidence to dye her hair any color she desired. But sometimes she did lack common sense. For instance, after her car was damaged a few times, I had to explain to her that when traffic is merging you should move over if you can. She laughed when I said that because she suddenly realized why drivers had flipped her off so often.

My friend's little silver car would zip around quickly. Once, she scraped the side of that car on the guardrail in downtown Dayton on an off ramp. The scrape ran all the way across and made this ear-numbing sound of metal on metal. Sparks flew. She laughed the entire time.

This woman could not understand the Midwest fascination with putting clothes on front porch ducks. She was amazed and laughed every time we drove through our neighborhood and saw how people would actually change the clothes on their ducks for different holidays. One night, she decided that the duck across the street needed a change of clothing, so she crept across the street, up the porch steps, and gave that duck a different costume.

The next morning as we sat on our front porch swing, sipping our coffee and reading the paper, we patiently waited for the neighbor to come out. He came onto the porch, walked down the stairs, grabbed his newspaper, walked back up the stairs—past the duck—entered the house and closed the door. Then he came right back out. After he looked around to see if anyone was watching, he reached down to rip off the duck's black bra and panties.

We laughed so hard . . . and then my roommate realized that she had lost her favorite bra and panties. She could never ask for them back.

* * *

When I was at Wright Patterson Air Force Base, one of my coworkers in the blood bank came from southern Alabama. He was a guy with a great sense of humor and a beautiful singing voice. Once he learned I grew up near Elwood, Indiana, he loved to give me a hard time, saying, "What would your daddy do if you came home with a boy as black as me?" He knew about our area because of KKK activity.

On one occasion, he was assigned to the upstairs "drawing room" when a white man came in who said he needed to have bloodwork done, but he didn't want any n----- touching him.

The young lady working in the drawing room was a young African-American Airman Basic. This statement shook her up. She walked back to the blood bank to catch her breath. Daryl—who outranked us all—simply said, "I'll draw him."

We wondered what would happen. We followed Daryl up front and watched as he entered the room. The look on the gentleman's face was priceless. Not only was Daryl extremely dark skinned, he was also very tall. Daryl turned on the charm . . . with the biggest smile and jolliest personality. He killed that man with kindness.

The best part was when he had the needle in the guy's arm. Without looking at him, he said, "Don't you ever use that word again." Darrell finished up, put a Band-Aid on, and told the gentleman to have a nice day. That man left in silence. Hopefully, he left with a changed perspective.

Leslie Coats Bales began her military career in 1978 when, at seventeen years old, she joined the United States Air Force. She served six years and achieved the rank of staff sergeant. In addition, she became the first female to qualify as a C5-A Loadmaster with the 301st Military Airlift Command, homebased at Travis AFB, California.

MY AIR FORCE STORY

LESLIE BALES

Taking His Lead

ONE OF MY EARLIEST RECOLLECTIONS was wishing I'd been born a boy. Why boys could wear pants to school but girls couldn't was beyond me. California may be known for its warm weather, but the bitter cold of Napa Valley mornings bore down on my bare legs as I walked the ten blocks to school. In 1972 when I entered sixth grade, the rules changed. Girls were finally permitted to play and dress like boys. I traded in my hand-made dresses for jeans from the annual church rummage sale.

Most mothers in my neighborhood stayed at home raising children. Mine was an exception. A skilled seamstress, she took a job at a fabric store not long after my brother, sister, and I entered middle school. Within a few years she had worked her way into the assistant store manager position. As the first female manager at Vallejo Hancock Fabrics, she paved the way for other women, setting an example I would one day follow.

My father, on the other hand, was a blue collar worker like most men at the shipyard. He was an industrial welder building our nation's elite nuclear-powered submarine force. Before marrying my mother, he served four years in the U.S. Army, working in intelligence, but it was toward the Navy that he felt a special connection. The tragic loss of the USS Thresher that sank during sea trials on April 10, 1963 never strayed far from his mind. Not only was I born the day it launched, my father worked aboard the submarine just months before it set sail. What was supposed to be the most advanced attack submarine of its kind lay in pieces 220 miles east of Cape Cod at the bottom of the ocean. The formation of ice in the high-pressure air pipes was suspected as the likely cause of its demise. To this day, the sinking of the USS Thresher remains the worst submarine disaster of its kind. The entire Navy community was devastated when 129 crew members and shipyard workers perished that day. Everyone that worked aboard the submarine felt some responsibility, including my father.

When I contemplated joining the service, it wasn't my dad's military background that drove me to enlist, but my desire to emulate my older brother. Our childhood growing up in the suburbs of Northern California was fairly typical: we ate dinner at the dinner table, attended church on Sundays, and after school my brother, younger sister and I played football and baseball until long after the sun went down. Whether it was a board game, ball game, or who had the longest French fry, we competed in almost everything. My competitive nature drove me to be like my older brother, but as a young girl that was an unbelievably difficult task, for Ted was good at everything he did, from academics to photography to archery. Although he was just one year my senior, he had privileges my younger sister and I only dreamed of. How could having a penis mean late nights, Friday night football games, and camp outs? But it did, and the injustice of that drove us to prove that girls should be treated equally. It drove us to excel, which we did both academically and on the ball fields.

In 1977, at sixteen years old, I graduated from my junior year at Vintage High School. I detested the girl drama of high school and did all I could to avoid it by taking college courses at night and working weekends. My parents supported my decision to graduate early, and after graduation the whole world lay before me . . . like a corn maze. I was uncertain which path to take. I felt totally free for the first time yet terrified for I had no idea which route to take, what to do with my life. College was an option. I could graduate with a degree before I turned twenty. But I was sick of school—despised it, in fact. I'd taken several odd jobs here and there, but after one week shucking avocados at a sub sandwich shop, I knew I had to do more with my life. Perhaps it was a sense there was more for me out there or just learning that my brother was off on his next new adventure . . . but soon after hearing of his enlistment with the United States Air Force, I found myself walking into the local recruiting office.

Each office of the armed forces lined a small strip mall not far from the front gates of the shipyard where my father worked. I hesitated about where to start, but the sharply dressed soldier with the tailored green uniform, shiny brass buttons, and rows of colorful ribbons caught my eye. As I listened to his pitch, he reminded me of the used car salesman that my dad and I talked to several months back when Dad co-signed the loan for my first car.

"So what are my options if I were to join?" I asked the Army sergeant.

"Well, it really depends on your ASVAB score."

"ASVAB score?"

"It's a series of tests that the services use to determine which MOS we can put you in."

"What's an MOS?"

"It means Military Occupational Specialties. They are the different career fields in the Army," he said as he handed me a basic training book.

After perusing the images of combat troops in training, I asked, "How soon can I take the ASVAB test?"

"Be here tomorrow at 1000 hours, and I'll take you over to the testing station."

I had a tough time sleeping that night. Young women in fatigues crawling under barbed wire and carrying rifles trekked through my mind. A soldier— could I really be a soldier? The Army recruiter said women would never be permitted in war zones, but how could I be sure? What could I actually do with my military skills after I got out? While I felt uneasy, the prospect of shucking avocados overruled that uneasiness.

My ASVAB results came back quickly. Unlike my brother, who scored so well he could choose any career he wanted, I found my options far more limited. I don't know if it was my actual score, or if the Army just didn't want women in meaningful jobs. The Army offered me positions as a food service specialist or supply technician; but neither option sounded appealing. After I refused to make a decision with the Army, my recruiter surprised me by suggesting I speak with the Air Force. While my options there weren't a whole lot better, I found one job that was not as a cook or a paper pusher and that I felt I could do. As an Air Cargo Specialist, I would build pallets, operate forklifts, and load heavy equipment onto airplanes—not your typical female job, which is what intrigued me most about it.

The next day I asked my parents to sign the waiver allowing me to enlist as a seventeen year old. In lieu of the four-year active duty commitment my brother made, I enlisted for six years in the USAF Reserves. While I was ready for an adventure, I wasn't quite ready to completely leave the familiarity and safety of my hometown. Two weeks after my brother left for boot camp, I followed.

Boot Camp—Lackland AFB

UNLIKE MOST NEW RECRUITS WHO left from Military Enlistment Personnel Stations (MEPS), I was driven by my parents to the airport. At San Francisco International, tears streamed down my face as I boarded the plane for boot camp. Embarking into the unknown terrified me, but by this point it was too late to turn back. I'd signed the papers and my recruiter made it clear there was no turning back. Once I arrived in San Antonio, Texas, a bus picked me up and my indoctrination to military life began.

"If you think you are good enough for my Air Force, think again you scum bags!" the drill instructor shouted at us "rainbows"—new recruits not yet issued uniforms. "Shoulders back. . . . Stand straight, you worthless piece of shit. You don't belong in my fucking Air Force."

"Oh, my God, what did I get myself into?" I thought as I struggled to follow every instruction.

Despite years of playing competitive sports, I quickly learned I was badly out of shape. Within days, not only did every muscle in my entire body ache from all the calisthenics, my arms hurt so badly from the inoculations I could barely lift them above my head.

It's odd that the Air Force spent so much effort creating strong, athletic airmen, yet they rewarded those that smoked cigarettes by allowing regular smoke breaks. Even if they didn't smoke, some took it up just so they could take a break from the often menial tasks of cleaning the barracks or putting foot lockers in order. I never missed an opportunity for a smoke break, a bad habit that made completing the obstacle course more difficult.

There was a lot I didn't understand. How did hours spent marching in circles on the parade grounds or rolling nylons into perfect "jelly rolls" make you a better airman? I would learn that it was the Air Force way of teaching us to follow instructions—instructions that if we were ever to go into battle would help keep us safe. Fortunately, I never had to follow battle commands since my six years in the military took place during peace time. In boot camp I learned to stay in step, render the perfect salute, master the obstacle course, and the importance of the US Air Force core values and traditions.

The first time I saw my brother was the last week of training at the base chapel on Sunday morning. From across the sanctuary, I could tell that the lanky kid with long hair I grew up with had been replaced with someone I barely recognized. Almost all the male recruits looked the same with their sharply-pressed uniforms, spit-shined boots, and military head gear that hid their freshly shaven heads, but Ted stood out—and not just because of his 6'4" height. His uniform already featured a single row of ribbons, along with the first airman's stripe he earned by completing Coast Guard boot camp three months earlier. He quickly learned that Coast Guard life on the water was not for someone who gets seasick so he transferred branches of service.

While he had changed, I had, too. I had definitely grown stronger physically, but the mental transformation was difficult to understand. Had I changed at my own will or because of the insistent droning from my drill instructors? Regardless, I had grown and was ready for the next phase of my military training.

Technical Training – Sheppard AFB

TECHNICAL TRAINING TOOK MY BROTHER and me in separate directions. Ted headed east, six hundred miles to Biloxi, Mississippi, where fried catfish, hushpuppies, and coleslaw found their way into the Keesler AFB chow halls. I traveled north 350 miles to Wichita, Texas, where barb-b-cue, corn-on-the-cob, and apple pie were favorite dishes in the Sheppard AFB chow halls. Fear of tornadoes replaced my apprehension of California earthquakes. Training went relatively well. I learned how to operate the winches and tie-downs that properly secured cargo. We spent hours perfecting our basic math skills. A lot of calculations went into determining how to properly balance an airplane so that it didn't take a nose dive when it took off. Personal computers did not exist back then, but hand calculators did. The Air Force, however, wanted everyone capable of performing the calculations without any technical assistance.

Unlike at boot camp, nights here were free, though occasionally I had homework. I spent many nights at the airman's club, sharpening my skills on the pool table. In fact, I celebrated my eighteenth birthday at the club. Late nights made it a struggle to stay awake in the classroom. You didn't want to doze off or you'd suffer consequences. If you were smart, you would stand in the back of the classroom if you felt sleepy—to make sure you stayed awake. But, though I had lots of free time, there was still structure. We had to assemble at 0630 and collectively march to the chow hall. At 0650 we then marched to our training rooms. We always carried three meticulously folded 341 Excellence/Discrepancy Reports in the front pocket of our fatigues in the event we got into trouble. While the forms were supposed to be used for highlighting accomplishments, I only saw it used to discipline airmen. I managed to get through Basic Training without having a 341 pulled and had only one pulled in Technical Training—for failing to report to formation on time.

At our boot camp graduation, Ted and I had agreed to meet after Technical Training to fly home together. I felt a tremendous sense of pride as we headed home on the plane. The teenager that left California feeling fearful of what lay ahead was coming back, confident and self-assured.

Osan, Korea

Summer Tour 1978

MY AIR FORCE OBLIGATION REQUIRED reporting for duty at Travis AFB in Fairfield, California, one weekend a month and two weeks in the summer. Twelve months into my Air Force commitment, I was selected to serve my first of many overseas assignments. I was one of fifteen reservists sent to Osan Air Base in South Korea to hone skills to ensure our units' preparedness should the United States ever go to war.

Technical Sergeant "Johnson" led my team. He'd been to Korea on multiple occasions, and when we landed, he suggested that, after checking into the barracks and stowing our gear, we go into town for dinner. After the long, twenty-plus-hour trip, many older reservists opted not to go, but at nineteen, I was excited to experience the local culture. Osan looked similar to military bases on U.S. soil, but as I approached the front gate into Songtan, I was struck by the filth and stench. The acrid scent of *kimchi* (a fermented vegetable dish), the odor of the open sewer system, and the reek of the fly-infested carcasses that hung from the open windows of meat shops overwhelmed me. Children approached us as we exited the post, begging for anything we could offer: candy, food, or a few *won*. Cars drove on the wrong side of the road, dodging bicyclists and pedestrians. Once we reached the restaurant, the menu items were indistinguishable, like chicken scratches in the sand. I had never eaten anything but your basic meat and potato dishes and had no desire to experiment. With help from my fellow servicemen, I ordered pizza, only to find Korean pizza looks and tastes nothing like American pizza. The round pie consisted of spicy red hot peppers, cabbage, and some unrecognizable vegetables. After one bite, I decided I would take the remainder of my meals at the base chow hall.

My assignment was building cargo pallets in the warehouse. I enjoyed the work but did not appreciate the extra attention I was getting from TSgt. Johnson, a married father of two, who evidently thought that being away in a foreign country gave him permission to break his wedding vows. I did my best to avoid him, but when two members of our group were selected to go to Seoul on a USO-sponsored tour of the DMZ, he and I were the ones chosen. I almost turned this once-in-a-lifetime opportunity down, but instead, I made it clear to him that I had absolutely no interest in his advances. While I thought I'd made myself clear, that night I was awakened at 0200 by loud pounding on my barracks door.

"Airman Coats, you got a phone call," someone shouted from the other side of my barracks door.

"What are you talking about?"

"There's a phone down the hall. Someone is on the phone for you." After I digested what was being said, I threw my fatigues and a T-shirt on and dashed down the hall.

"This is Airman Coats."

"You fucking bitch, who do you think you are? You're nothing but a whore," a man in an obviously inebriated state slurred into the phone.

Without a word, I slammed down the phone and ran back to my room. I was mad. No, I was more than mad. I knew who it was, but I was young, naïve, and too afraid to tell anyone. I did my best to go back to sleep, but the pounding in my chest made it impossible. When I reported the next morning for my trip to Seoul, I was pleased to see that another woman, a lieutenant colonel, would be joining us. Her presence averted some of the sergeant's relentless pressure for me to be with him. I did everything I could to avoid TSgt. Johnson. If we had to be in the same room, I made certain I was on the opposite side. When the suggestion of having dinner in Seoul was brought up, I pretended I wasn't feeling well. Perhaps he realized the stupidity of his actions, or he figured out there was no way his advances would go anywhere. Eventually, he quit bothering me.

Once we arrived at Yongsan, the Air Force facility in Seoul, we were ushered into a special briefing room. The first sergeant quickly reviewed a list of do's and don'ts for the tour: Do not smile. Do not show the bottom of your shoes. Do not wave when addressing North Koreans. All of these were a cultural faux pas. We were then handed a piece of paper to sign. After reading the list of do's and don'ts of the tour, I read the final paragraph: "The visit to the Joint Security Area at Panmunjom will entail entry into a hostile area and the possibility of injury or death as a direct result of enemy action. I recognize if I am injured or killed while at the DMZ, I will not hold the government of the United States responsible."

"Wow, what am I getting myself into?" I wondered. But I trusted my government would protect me so I signed the document and boarded the bus along with the others in the group. We first visited the Bridge of No Return, a small, one-lane, concrete bridge used for prisoner exchanges at the end of the Korean War. While the bridge still stands, the last prisoners known to have crossed it were the eighty-two crew members of the USS Pueblo. These U.S. servicemen were captured off the coast of North Korea on January 23, 1968, and held for eleven months. When they were released, they were told never to return.

We were then taken to the Joint Security Area, which consisted of a row of blue buildings used during the signing of the Armistice Agreement that ended the Korean War. The armed North and South Korean soldiers that surrounded the building were a stark reminder of the historic landmark. Surprisingly, the room was not much larger than a typical American living room. The building's artifacts, such as the flags and old wooden tables, were the cause of many disagreements during the peace talks that took more than two years to complete. I made a point of remaining extra vigilant to my surroundings while keeping all the do's and don'ts in mind.

When I looked out the window and saw a North Korean soldier closely watching me, I became nervous. I tried to ignore his stare, but eventually our eyes met, and when they did, a wide grin spread across his face and I could see the secret offering of a wave that he hid, in the most discrete way possible, from his fellow comrades. It was hard not to smile at that. While we were warned of the North Korean culture, he must have been warned of American culture. It warmed my heart to see him try to connect in this small way.

Anchorage, Alaska

IN FEBRUARY 1979, I EMBARKED on my second overseas tour of duty. It was a three-month detail to Clark AFB, a U.S. military base outside of Angeles City, Philippines. But first, I was assigned to a two-week detail in the sub-zero temperatures of Anchorage, Alaska.

When I arrived at Elmendorf AFB, I arrived in full, Air Force issued, cold-weather gear. Good thing because it was downright frigid. As an Air Cargo Specialist, I could be assigned to any of the following jobs: building pallets and operating forklifts in the warehouse; uploading, downloading, and safely securing cargo; working in the Air Traffic Control Office; or providing aircraft fleet (sanitary) services. Fleet services was my least preferred job primarily because it meant working outside in sub-zero temperatures. But the fact you spent the shift emptying shitters all day also made it less appealing than other jobs. Unfortunately, fleet services was the job I was assigned. Like a good airman, I saluted and did what I was told. The mukluks and parka kept me warm, as long as I kept the cord of my hood scrunched tight. While I sat in the warmth of the water truck, the civil servant who I was assigned to help did most of the work. Given the freezing temperature, I was relieved to not have to go outside. The civil servants often considered reservists more of a burden than an aid. My colleague, however, did appreciate my ability to play pinochle, a game my father and uncle taught me as a young girl. There weren't many planes leaving in the middle of the night, so we spent many hours playing cards until we were called to prepare a plane for departure.

After five days of duty, I earned two days of liberty. My brother was stationed at Murphy Dome, a long-range radar site, twenty miles west of Fairbanks, Alaska, which provided a way for our military career paths to cross once again in an exciting way. Although the forty-eight hours of liberty provided sufficient time to make the six-hour drive by car, the weather conditions forbade it. When the locals learned my brother was in Fairbanks, my new civil servant friends made a call.

"Sgt. Harris, this is Kevin Miller. Is the daily run up to Fairbanks still on schedule for tomorrow morning?"

"Hey, Kev, yeah, what's going on?"

"I got an Airman reservist here on her two-week tour of duty who has a brother stationed at Murphy Dome. Do you think you can get her on tomorrow's run up to Fairbanks?"

"As long as General Davis doesn't need it. Just have her here at the terminal at 0700 and if it's a go, we'll get her on it."

"Fantastic, I owe you, buddy."

When I arrived at the terminal, I was relieved to learn the flight was still a go. The C-12 was a huge departure from the side facing web seats of the C-130 that took five, long, uncomfortable hours to get from California to Alaska. I was amazed that no sooner had we reached cruising altitude than we began our descent into Fairbanks.

Ted had been in Alaska almost a year with very few visitors. Due to the top-secret nature of his work, family or friends would never know the work he did. Because of my military status and the security clearance I held, I was at least able to tour the highly secure facility. As we pulled into the Communication Station at Murphy Dome, we provided our military IDs to the guard, who quickly raised the security bar, allowing us entry. I immediately saw why they called the station a dome. There were four large domes peeking out from under the deep snow. Little did I anticipate that there was a complete underground community with a bowling alley, base exchange, chapel, and living quarters.

We followed the path to an entrance that appeared to be the only way in and out of the building. Ted swiped his badge across the security locks, and the doors clicked open. As he escorted me through the building, he highlighted the various features of the facility. When we entered the largest dome where he spent a majority of his time, it was like walking onto a movie set. Across the far side of the dome there were six massive TV screens that displayed a world map. On the other side, in theater fashion, were multiple rows of workstations similar to a NASA Launch Control Station. Ted pointed out that the various shapes and dots on the jumbo screens represented aircraft currently in the air, but he would not divulge what they actually did with the information. I sensed the work he did was very important to the security of our nation.

After finishing the tour, we headed back to his home in Fairbanks. Our time together did not last long, but we took advantage of every minute we had. We stayed up late into the night catching up—talking about friends from high school, how our parents and little sister were doing, and how life in the Air Force had changed us since we were last together at boot camp. It was strange to see Ted in this unusual environment with a new job and a new wife. Although we'd lived together in the same house for nearly two decades, he was different. He was still my big brother; however, he was no longer the person I strived to beat, but someone I admired—someone I loved. When the sun arose, he had to take me back to the terminal, and I flew back to Anchorage to finish my detail.

My Flight Log

THE THICK BLACK COVER WITH embossed gold letters, now faded, is a reminder of the most adventurous time of my life. The pages mean little to most: SUU, HIK, OKO, KUV, acronyms only someone on a flight crew will understand. They remind me of flights to Spain, England, Germany, Japan, and many other countries. They bring back an adventurous time, the kind few women experienced in the early 1980s.

The log reminds me of courageous and memorable times in the air, such as my first trip when the front landing gear would not come down and the rough ride over the North Atlantic for my first and only mid-air refueling trip. The log brings back long conversations I had with many servicemen and women or retirees off on their own adventures.

It's a reminder of daring times on foreign soil; of eating sticks of meat, having asked for beef or pork, and wondering if I was eating monkey or dog; of trying to communicate with foreign nationals who struggled to understand English; and, oh my favorite, of throwing a beer bottle through the back windshield of a car, though a story too long to tell here.

The log is a reminder of a time that I may one day share with my granddaughter, who already displays a fearlessness that makes her grandmother smile.

Clark AFB, Philippines

IT'S BEEN SAID THAT COCKROACHES would survive a nuclear apocalypse. When molten ash spewed from the mouth of Mount Pinatubo on June 17, 1991, shooting twenty million tons of sulfur dioxide into the atmosphere, it sent to their deaths the descendants of a giant cockroach I met ten years earlier. Clark Air Force Base looked much different in the early 1980s when I accepted a three-month detail. Then it was home to tropical vegetation and all types of wildlife. The base was also a central supply hub used during the Vietnam War and, while the war had ended years earlier, U.S. aircraft routinely flew in and out of Clark.

I was assigned to Air Traffic Control, a job for which leadership skills were needed. Instead of having specific tasks handed to me, I was given the responsibility to ensure all inbound and outbound flights were properly serviced. As a representative for the base commander, I worked the flight line—meeting planes on their arrival and making certain the crew had everything they needed prior to departure. I developed communication skills while working with all levels of the chain of command, and eventually my confidence began to soar. I took incoming calls into the Command Center while making the appropriate changes to the white board. When the loadmaster was ready to receive the outbound cargo, I'd get on the radio and direct the air cargo specialist to deliver the load. When there were problems with fleet services, I'd direct crews to return to the aircraft. This confidence allowed me to confront a pilot and crew when their plane landed with cargo that was bug-ridden by unidentified insects. When I informed the crew that they would have to depart the aircraft and it would be sealed until the load could be investigated, they were not happy and initially refused to exit the plane. I calmly explained that my orders were coming directly from the base commander and, if they would like, I'd gladly take them to him and they could express their displeasure directly to the commander. They gathered their gear and exited the aircraft.

When I wasn't pounding the scorching pavement of the tarmac, I lived off base in a cockroach-infested hotel in Angles City. My cousin, LaDessa, an avionics technician, was also stationed at Clark living in the same hotel. As two female Staff Sergeants, both 5'10" with the same last name stitched over the pocket of our uniforms, we stood out. In fact, wherever we went people stared. While I grew up in the suburbs of northern California, LaDessa, the daughter of a U.S. Forest Officer, grew up in the Sierra Nevada Mountains. I was disgusted by the huge cockroaches that roamed the hotel and about every inch of the country, but LaDessa wasn't fazed. These weren't your everyday American cockroaches, not that those couldn't gross someone out. The average size of a cockroach in the Philippines is about two to three inches long. We could be walking down the sidewalk and there'd be so many cockroaches we couldn't help but step on them. But, as I mentioned, LaDessa wasn't upset. When we'd return to our hotel, she would scour my room looking for those filthy critters and when she inevitably found one or two, she'd carefully pick them up with her bare hands and release them outside the confines of my room.

One morning, after an 1800 to 0600 shift, the day's heat was rising and I returned to my room to try to sleep with no air conditioning. Unfortunately, my cousin wasn't with me. I quickly scanned the room relieved to find it seemed clear of any bugs. I donned my sleeping attire—a white T-shirt over a bikini I purchased from a recent trip to Greece. Not long after I'd fallen asleep, I awoke. Sitting atop my pillow, inches from my face, was the biggest, ugliest cockroach I had ever seen, staring me in the eyes. Yikes! I jumped out of bed, grabbed my room key, and flew upstairs to sleep on a lounge chair beside the pool.

That was not my first close encounter with a critter while stationed at Clark. After checking into my hotel on my first day of arrival, I'd carefully laid my uniform out in preparation for the first day on the job. When I awoke the next morning and turned on the light, I found a green lizard crawling over my freshly pressed uniform. The bright lights startled him as much as he startled me, and he scurried up my bedroom wall. Shaking uncontrollably, I quickly undressed and, without waiting for the water to warm, got into the cold ceramic-tiled shower. My eyes scanned every inch of the shower the entire time I showered in fear that the lizard would come looking for me. Once out, I grabbed another not so freshly pressed uniform, put it on as quickly as I could, threw my wet hair in a bun, skipped the make-up, slapped on a hat, and dashed out the room. When I reported for duty, I realized I'd forgotten my belt and had on one black sock and one blue sock. My colleagues found my story amusing as the locals considered the little geckos a sign of good luck. During my three-month stay in the Philippines I began to appreciate the geckos and welcomed their good fortune. The cockroaches, on the other hand, will always disgust me.

My work shift consisted of two ten-hour days from 6 p.m.-6 a.m., two days from 6 a.m.-6 p.m., and then I had three days off. This gave me plenty of off-duty time to shoot pool at the enlisted club, snorkel with friends in Subic Bay, and enjoy the nightlife in Angeles City. For a few pesos, I could buy the perfect meal: a stop at one of the roadside stands would procure me my main course—meat-on-a-stick. I'd ask for chicken, pork, or beef, but I never really knew what I was eating. The best part of my meal was the warm, flaky biscuits that melted in my mouth; young boys sold them from small baskets off the back of their bicycles. To top the meal off, I'd drink a bottle of San Miguel beer.

One such meal proved to be very interesting . . . on the verge of dangerous. After a girlfriend and I had finished eating, we began walking back with our beer in-hand toward our hotel. A red car with four American GIs pulled up and asked us to go for a ride. It quickly became clear that the guys were wasted as the smoke and smell of marijuana poured out of the car. Their vulgar advances were almost threatening, so we told them we weren't interested and to get lost. The driver peeled away, spinning his tires and sending gravel flying into our faces. With skilled precision from my many years of fast pitch softball,

I threw my beer bottle at the vehicle. The impact shattered the back window and sent glass everywhere. Immediately afterwards, my friend threw her bottle. Once we saw the taillights of the vehicle come on, we ran, hiding alongside a house. With my heart pounding, I heard a Filipino man step out of his house shouting. We couldn't understand what he was saying, but we knew he didn't appreciate the ruckus going on. Dogs barked loudly, and we were certain we'd created a lot of trouble for ourselves. Eventually, the man went back into the house and a few minutes later, feeling the coast was clear, we slipped out from between the houses and into a nearby bar in hopes of finding someone that could make sure we got back to our quarters safely.

A bar right outside a military installation wasn't hard to find. After we shared our story with GIs sitting at the bar, our newly acquired friends offered to walk us back to our hotel. We hadn't gone two blocks when the familiar red vehicle once again appeared. We could see the men who'd made the earlier advances brushing broken glass off of the trunk. Not wanting any more trouble, we blended in with the group of GIs and walked right past them. When we finally made it back to the hotel, I breathed a huge sigh of relief and vowed I would not let myself get into another precarious situation.

The rest of my tour went relatively smoothly. I stayed away from town and spent more time on base, focusing on my military responsibilities. By the end of my reserve duty, I had made a lot of friends and developed leadership skills that would prepare me for greater responsibility down the road. A reward for a job well done was a first-class trip home on a commercial flight, compliments of the base commander.

Survival Training

IT WAS 1982 AND I had spent the last eight months of my life living out of a suitcase as I crisscrossed the globe. One week I was dining in a quaint restaurant in Rhoda, Spain, and the next, standing atop the Acropolis in Athens amid the ruins of the Parthenon. Weeks later I was snorkeling in Subic Bay in the clear, Persian-blue waters of the South China Sea. I had logged many hours in my flight log, and the only thing keeping me from becoming the first female loadmaster in my command to pin aircrew wings was completing Survival, Evasion, Resistance, and Escape (SERE) training.

I delayed survival training as long as I could because the horror stories were worrisome. My fellow crew members were unrelenting in their teasing, telling me how I would be forced to eat live bugs and undergo torturous interrogation techniques and brutal days in the wilderness with little food. My way to avoid eating bugs was to complete survival training in February in the middle of the Cascade Mountains. I don't know what I was thinking. I traded in a meal of bugs for deep snow and bitter cold. While the Air Force provided the proper cold-weather gear, the sub-zero temperatures at night made it a challenge to stay warm.

Most students at SERE training were crewmembers, consisting of pilots, engineers, navigators, loadmasters, and crew chiefs. Occasionally intelligence officers and life support personnel attended as well. In a male-dominated field, the likelihood of being teamed with other women was slim. While there were two other women in training, our paths rarely crossed. I was teamed with six men, all significantly bigger and taller than me, with one exception—the lone officer. The lieutenant was out to prove himself. He did nothing half-ass. On the day of our escape and evasion drill, my team helped one another apply camo paint to our faces. We were then paired into teams of two. Of all the big, strong men that I could have been paired with, I got the slender lieutenant. I'm not sure who was more disappointed, he or I. Our orders were to get from checkpoint Alpha to checkpoint Charlie, without getting caught by the enemy. Everyone was eventually supposed to get caught, but the lieutenant had other plans. He and I double-timed the entire trek going far out of our way to ensure we did not get captured. We were the last team to make it to checkpoint Charlie; however, we successfully evaded all signs of the enemy. It's funny that thirty years later I do not recall a single name of the six men I survived survival training with, but the memories of that training are still vivid.

I remember how I sewed backpacks late into the night while thrusting the heavy needle into the thick canvas material until my fingers bled. After seeing all of the gear that I would be required to carry for a week in the mountains, I knew physically I could not bear the weight. I had to find other ways to be accepted by the team. So I sewed, I cooked, I cleaned and did not feel badly about it. I learned how to capitalize on the strengths of a team in order to reach a common goal. I learned survival techniques like compass reading, setting snares, and how to make beef jerky. I learned to never give up while climbing to the top of an eight-hundred-foot mountain, though with every four steps I took, I fell through the snow. How could the men on my team walk on top of four to five feet of snow, while I, seventy-five pounds lighter, fell through with almost every other step? The men were always supportive of me throughout training, and they drove me to reach the mountaintop as I dragged my pack behind me. When I finally reached it, we all celebrated. Nothing ever tasted as good as that MRE with its can of peaches.

Survival training prepared me to be a strong leader in a male-dominated field. It also made me more sensitive to the trials of servicemen and women who have served during wartime and undergone extreme deprivations or endured the unthinkable in prisoner of war camps. Their stories shake me to the core.

Air Force Meets Navy

WHEN MY SISTER'S FIANCÉ JOHN pointed out his buddy standing at the bar in the bib overalls, I was intrigued. He seemed certain of himself. Anyone wearing bib overalls without a shirt had to be self-assured . . . or full of himself. You didn't see that mid-western look too often in northern California, especially in a Marine bar. He looked as though he'd just spent the day loading hay. It was rather sexy. When he arrived at our table, I was taken in by his bright blue eyes, practically enamored with his good looks. My sister, Lisa, introduced me to Ron, a sailor who served on the USS Seawolf, the same boat where her fiancé served. While it may sound cliché, I knew from the moment Ron and I met that he was the man I would marry.

Initially our schedules rarely meshed. I was off on frequent trips maintaining my flight status, while his boat was off on top-secret missions he could never speak of. When we happened to be in port at the same time, we visited San Francisco, Sacramento, and Lake Tahoe, where we picnicked in the parks and went out for romantic dinners. Ron made me laugh. He and his buddies would come to me and my sister's ball games to watch us play. The USS Seawolf crew were our biggest fans, taunting the other teams and whooping and hollering whenever our team made a good play or had a solid hit.

Between Ron's sea duty and my flight time, the away times got more difficult as we fell in love. Eight months after we met, Ron asked me to marry him. It was nothing elaborate, unlike proposals of today. We wandered by a jewelry store while out shopping and, as we looked at the wedding rings, decided to buy a set. Eventually Ron asked my father for my hand in marriage. After he had picked up our rings, he got down on his knee in my parents' kitchen and officially asked me to marry him. While I was elated to begin planning our wedding, I began feeling the pressure of my responsibilities to maintain my flight status as a USAF reservist and Ron's desire to keep me at home. His jealousy threatened my independence, but I was in love. It was the early 1980s and not many women worked outside of their homes.

On our honeymoon I received a call from Mare Island Naval Shipyard offering me my first job in the civil service. I had the option of selecting from a number of apprentice positions: welder, pipe fitter, sheet metal fitter, among others. I selected the sheet metal apprentice job. While I was excited about the new opportunity, Ron was not in the least bit happy. He struggled envisioning his wife working aboard submarines in such close quarters with the same kind of men he lived with. I understood he really wanted to support my career aspirations, but I also knew he wasn't happy. When the Navy decided to send him to a three-month school at Great Lakes Naval Training Center in Chicago, I quit my job to be with him. That was not the first time I gave up a job to keep peace in my marriage.

His sea time and my flight time continued to be a challenge for us. Each time I would have to leave on a trip to maintain my reserve status, he complained. I became unhappy. Ultimately we agreed that should he get out of the Navy, and whenever I wanted to reenter the service, he would support me. That made my decision to leave the service easier. Since then, he has always been my strongest supporter of my career choices. While I never returned to the Air Force, I've had a long career as a civil servant supporting those who serve. Ron was thrilled that my career choices in the civil service were far less risky than my days in the Air Force. Not long after I left the service, we began our family and have been married thirty-four years.

How My Service Shaped Me

THIRTY-EIGHT YEARS AGO, WHEN I joined the Air Force, I was just a child of seventeen, not even old enough to vote. Though naïve, I felt fearless and wanted more out of my life than jumping from one minimum-wage job to another. The Air Force helped strengthen my character as I learned respect, accountability, and leadership. Developing a strong sense of self early in my career shaped me into the person I am today.

My first encounter in taking responsibility was in boot camp. After a long day on the obstacle course, the women in my squadron were winding down. Most had just taken showers; some were shining boots. A general sense of happiness prevailed as our training was nearing the end. I had just showered, and as I walked by my friend, I teased her with a high-karate kick, intending to show off my hand-to-hand combat skills. Unfortunately, my foot dislodged the bottle of nail polish remover from her hand and the bottle came crashing down. The liquid hit the floor in a large, acidic puddle that ate through twenty coats of floor polish in a matter of seconds. I was mortified. My team had spent the last five weeks buffing the floor so you could see your reflection. Now this puddle of faded tile sat staring at me, and I was the only person to blame.

I ran to the supply room and poured liquid wax over the spot. My fellow squad mates did all they could to help, but this was no easy fix. Even if I stayed up all night applying coats of wax, it would not have helped. I needed to confess, but it took all the courage I could muster. I reported my mistake to my drill instructor. Much to my surprise, he was empathetic; furthermore, he thanked me for facing my mistake and my fears head on. That experience taught me to take accountability for my actions and for the employees under my command. I learned to allow for mistakes, for through mistakes we grow.

In a memorable fashion, I came to understand the importance of my classroom lessons. I'd spent hours studying the chain of command, rank, and insignia as well as the proper method of addressing senior leaders. I learned about the core values of the Air Force: integrity first, service before self, and excellence in all we do. But, once I reported to duty and began working with all levels of the chain of command, I became lackadaisical. The strong working relationship I established with my first sergeant made it easy to talk to him. On one occasion, I walked into his office paying little attention to the gentleman with his back to me.

While I recognized they were in conversation, I interrupted them to request permission to run to the chow hall for lunch. The first sergeant, in a firm voice, suggested that I wait outside his office until he had finished his conversation with the commander. I immediately did an about-face, left the office, and then my heart sank. Apart from one slight mishap at boot camp, I'd never gotten in trouble before.

My first thought was, "How dare he." I was angry for the way he put me in my place. But during the twenty minutes I had to replay the incident over and over in my mind, I came to realize that I was wrong. When the commander finally exited the first sergeant's office, I apologized for my behavior. He kindly accepted my apology. The first sergeant, however, took the opportunity to help me learn from the experience. He reprimanded me for my behavior but in such a way that I could recover from the blunder with greater insight. This lesson still resonates today. When my children or staff make mistakes, I understand that it's important to praise them first in pubic and, if necessary, reprimand in private. My goal is for them to leave the situation knowing that one can recover from any mistake.

Finally, as a young loadmaster, I honed leadership skills as the hours racked up on my flight log. Once I received the passenger manifest and cargo details, I performed the calculations to determine the proper distribution of weight to ensure a safe take-off and landing. The order of cargo was relayed to the Air Cargo Team, and, upon its arrival to the aircraft, I would supervise the proper placement and securing of cargo. During flight I ensured the cargo stayed safe. There were many unique loads: helicopters, vehicles for top dignitaries, even human remains. Passengers, however, were the most important cargo. For them I performed tasks similar to those of a flight attendant, such as relaying egress procedures in the event of an emergency, preparing and delivering meals, providing any support they might need in flight. What I enjoyed the most were the lengthy conversations I had with the service men and women from all branches of service.

My time in the Air Force helped me grow up. While I was young and naive when I joined, I was strong and self-assured when I left. My experiences, both in the Air Force and as a Navy wife, help me today in my role as the Director for Customer Operations at the Defense Finance and Accounting Service (DFAS), where I serve over 6.5 million current and past servicemen and women. Each day I am driven to serve those who serve, something that I began to learn at the age of seventeen.

My Boots

Strong, thick laces
crisscrossed the front of my black,
spit-shined boots—
boots worn in the scorching heat,
pounding parade ground pavement,
trudging through the deep snow,
surviving survival school,
landing on many foreign soils,
committed to serve.
Boots donned by a young, naïve
17-year old girl,
removed by a strong,
self-assured woman.

Christylee Sparrow Hawk Vickers was nineteen years old when she enlisted for active duty in the U.S. Army in 2002. As a 63B10-Light Wheel Vehicle Mechanic, she was first stationed at the 21st TSC in Kaiserslautern, Germany. She then served with the 101st Airborne Division 3BDE, 3STB, HHC. She deployed to Iraq from September 2005 to March 2006. Because of the needs of the Army, she served an additional ten months after her enlistment contract ended with the Rank of SPC and up for a promotion.

Christylee Vickers

WHAT I KNOW OF WAR

CHRISTYLEE VICKERS

Yellow Ribbons

I SEE THEM STILL, THE yellow ribbons of my second grade year, tied to the Reserve Center's chain link fence. They represented country before self and the honor of military service. On the morning of September 11, 2001, as I watched a newscast of the attack on the Twin Towers, I felt the pull of those ribbons. I knew I would enlist and serve.

I come from a family of service members. Both of my grandfathers served as did their fathers before them. Grandpa O'Neal has proudly told us how each generation on his side of the family has served our country since the Civil War. My parents served, too, and even met in the Army at Ft. Bragg, North Carolina. My dad, as Active Army, did a tour in Germany before the Berlin Wall came down, and then he served in the Reserves until retirement. He deployed to the Persian Gulf War during Desert Storm and Desert Shield. My mother's service took place during the Cold War. I would beg her to show me pictures of herself in uniform, and because I longed for adventure and bravery, I would stash those few pictures away.

I would pester everyone in my family for details about their service. I learned that Grandpa O'Neal was a welder. My uncle was a medic. My dad worked in transportation and drove trucks, delivering everything from fuel to mail. My mom was a supply clerk. I particularly wanted to know what she did in the Army. Was it the same as the men? One story my mother told me made me laugh. Once when her unit was on a field training exercise she was put in charge of the radio at the main headquarters. After two days of receiving no messages and trying to contact my mom to no avail, someone in the unit drove to her location to find out why the radio wasn't working. She hadn't plugged it in!

My dad left for the Persian Gulf War when I was nine and in the second grade. I knew he was still in the Army Reserves, but I didn't comprehend that he could go to war. I didn't even know he was going until it was happening— till he was boarding a plane and heading off to protect Kuwait from the Iraqi Army. He flew off for the big desert of Saudi Arabia, where there were no trees and lots of sand. I had barely seen him after he and my mom divorced. We lived in different states, with the 73.6 mile gulf between our houses as wide and deep as the hurt in my heart.

I feared for my father, off to fight in a war that might mean his death. He took an oath that superseded family and all other obligations. Would my last memory of him be as one of the random faces the camera man took to fill time before the next CNN commercial? As a child I didn't understand the effects this war had on him. Only as a veteran myself do I have the heart-wrenching awareness of how war changed him.

In elementary school teachers and students treated me differently once the Persian Gulf War started. Teachers sometimes talked in hushed voices, and we sent things "for the Troops" or my dad.

I remember the day I received a letter with no stamp, just FREE written in the upper-right corner. It was from my dad, addressed to me on yellow paper from a legal pad. The words were in pencil, and there were doodles in the margins and on the envelope. To this day, I still have this letter.

In every deployment, every war, every conflict, call it what you will, soldiers write letters to the ones they love. I know I sent out a few myself. To those I tried to be strong for and protect from harsh reality, I wrote about the weather, food, scenery, and what a good day was. Only to a few did I ever allude to the real hell of war. Even in my personal journals I did my best to stay positive, writing about love and home.

As I watched the planes ram into the Twin Towers, I knew that I could no longer postpone the inevitable. My country needed me. But I still delayed. I spent my first semester of college educating myself on the historical conflict of the Middle East. I searched my soul and was ready to embrace the possibility of fighting in the same countries as my father.

During my first year of college, I enlisted, and that following summer I was on my way to Ft. Jackson, South Carolina, for Basic Training and AIT. I was going to be a helper and a fixer. Wasn't that the job of a soldier, after all? Wasn't the soldier there to stand up for the oppressed and protect them? I was going to do that. Females, I thought, weren't allowed to be close to enemy action. I figured I'd be safe from the bad stuff and could help with the good stuff. I wanted to be a soldier who interacted with the people and gained their trust.

Despite my family's strong history of patriotic duty, I didn't understand the real legacy of military service until after I enlisted and felt an overwhelming sense of belonging, camaraderie, and purpose. Everything we did each day was to prepare and keep us in battle-ready posture. I can also attest to the camaraderie between soldiers. In war, the bonds of friendship strengthen as you face the possibility of losing comrades you love. Later, I didn't know the depths of pain and loss until I was a veteran and given the boot from my unit.

Learning My Job

LEARNING TO BE A 63B-LIGHT Wheel Vehicle Mechanic was truly an experience I shall never forget. I chose this job skill based on my ASVAB (Armed Services Vocational Assessment Battery) score as well as the cash bonus I would receive for learning said job and the assurance that it would send me to Europe for my first Duty Assignment.

In AIT (Advanced Individual Training) I was one of six females in our class of sixty from Alpha Company. I was also as green and new to the maintenance program as the BDU uniform I wore. I had no idea how anything mechanical worked. Fortunately, the TMs (Technical Manuals) were written at an eighth grade reading level, with detailed diagrams, flowcharts, and step-by-step instruction.

Each week we learned about a specific system in the vehicle family: engine, transmission, electrical, brakes, suspension, etc. On Monday through Thursday, after classroom time, we received three hours of hands-on troubleshooting, diagnosis, and repair instruction. If you failed Friday's test on that block of instruction, you could retake it once before being recycled and put into another class. Some people did fail, but it was because of their own pride or laziness. We were allowed to use the TMs for our testing, but we had to know which one we needed and go to the front of the room to ask for it. We could also use all the notes that could fit on a 5x7 index card. We could even ask the instructor three yes or no questions.

Unlike the guys, I didn't have any problem with pride. The instructors liked that I was willing to ask questions or find the answers in a book. They didn't mind if I asked what might sound like a stupid question. When our instructor presumed we knew how to fill a battery with water, I asked how to do that. None of my classmates knew the answer either, but they hadn't the nerve to ask. The instructor's respectful response to my battery question gave me confidence to keep asking questions. Our instructors said it was easier to teach a female soldier to do the job the right way once than to break the guys of their bad habits.

My friendship with the guys—my brothers in arms—is worth mentioning. A group of us, about ten, would pitch in for hotel rooms during our Off Post Pass weekends. When I was in a drunken state, they'd chase off anyone flirting with me and safely deposit me into the hotel bed. I would wake up with the guys sleeping along the bed edge or on the floor by the bed to make sure no one bothered me. These brothers had my back.

When I read my journal from that time, I realize how lucky I was to have a group of friends like these. And, yes, I took care of them, too. I played the role of mother hen. I'd bring up as much of the continental breakfast as I could carry. I would write reminder notes for them on what to study and what TMs to look at. It helped that these guys saw me as an equal and that when they looked at me, they saw their sisters or mother back home.

Home Is Where the Army Sends You

WHEN IT WAS TIME TO find out where our first duty stations would be, I stood in formation certain of where I was headed. I chose "Duty Station of

Choice, Europe" when I enlisted, which meant just one thing, Germany. So when the drill sergeant handed out our Orders by name, while telling us how vital this sheet of paper was, I was aghast. KOREA. But there it was alongside my name and SSN. It was impossible to get the drill sergeant's attention; he was too busy talking about the virtues of being chosen to go to Air Assault and Airborne School and details from his favorite duty stations.

"Drill Sergeant, I'm not supposed to go to Korea! Drill Sergeant." I sounded off when a moment opened up for questions.

"What do you mean? You go where the Army sends you," he said, slightly put off that I didn't want to be "queen for a year," which is what women serving in Korea were called. I wanted to go to Germany because that's where my dad had served and in school I had studied German language, history, and culture.

"But, Drill Sergeant, I enlisted for Europe, for Germany, and I can prove it. I have my contract," I mustered, knowing full well that my outburst might mean push-ups. Yet standing there at Parade Rest, sharp elbows V-ed out, and my palms moist with South Carolina heat, I sensed his interest in my last statement. I brought my contract because my dad told me to. I brought my contract because I heard one too many horror stories of "breach of contract" and "if only." I knew that if you can prove something legally, you have a leg to stand on.

"If you really do have your enlistment contract with you, bring it to my office when we get back to the barracks," the sergeant said before we marched onward toward the physicals and shots some of us would need to go overseas.

Later that evening, after mail call when we were to prep our uniforms for the next day, I went with my battle buddy down the hall to the drill sergeant's office. I never before noticed the darkness of this hallway, but the gloom seemed to intensify my resolve to not back down. I would get what I signed up for.

"Never put your name on it, unless you really know what you're getting yourself into," I could hear Grandpa remind me whenever I'd ask why he was writing another letter to the editor, a company who didn't follow through, or the State Attorney General. I remember Grandpa writing a lot of letters about integrity and keeping your word. I silently offered up thanks to my grandpa for making me promise to read every word of my contract before I signed it.

When I handed over my enlistment contract and snapped back to Parade

Rest, I feared the drill sergeant would laugh and rip it up. So only when he made a copy of the pages signed and initialed "Duty Station of Choice/Europe" could I relax.

This was my first experience of standing up against a system that could exploit my lack of knowledge if I didn't learn how to educate myself on the workings of its cluster-fuck of moving pieces. Others might have just accepted defeat, but I said, "No, you can't deny me my right." I had information at hand and resources at the ready just like I had been taught while learning how to fix military vehicles. To troubleshoot a problem, you need to find the best approach. You need to be willing to ask for help and not hang back in fear of defeat.

Breaking Rank

AFTER TWO YEARS OF SERVING as an Army mechanic in Germany, an experience I greatly enjoyed, I am deployed to Iraq with the 101st Airborne Division. Iraq is where I learn what it's like to face hours of mortar shells that shake the walls. Iraq is where I have my first breakdown.

We are standing in formation when we are told we won't be at Forward Operating Base Speicher until New Year, 2006. That means two more weeks at FOB Summerall. Unable to keep it together anymore, I break ranks and run to the room set aside for females. It is already empty of belongings since they have been sent ahead to Speicher. I cry loud and hard, so hard my body shakes. My sobs echo through the warehouse we use as a multipurpose building. My wails must reach the laundry, showers, sleeping quarters, motor pool, and my Company HQ.

No one comes in until I am a spent shell. Then Chica arrives to see if I need water. The staff sergeant and sergeant first class come to tell me they are disappointed that I have lost my military bearing. They say I need to "embrace the suck" of deployments just like everyone else.

I have truly done it. After a year with the Rakkassans and my unit, I have proven the prejudice against women in uniform correct. I'm not made for war. December's monthly counseling statement states that I don't act as I did when we first arrived. I am depressed, but they don't agree that I need to be sent to Mental Health just yet. It is noted that my mood appeared noticeably depressed after our most recent mortaring that took two lives—*Jimmie L. Shelton* and *Thomas C. Skiekert.*

Their deaths and the rattling of buildings, the dust, and blood-splattered walls haunt me. I have been using so much energy to keep myself together and now the one light on the horizon—getting to Speicher—is gone. Getting to Speicher is everything. It is the reason I keep moving forward, why I push through. Speicher is where my fiancée is, where his unit is, where my few friends are. More than anything, I want to not feel so empty and alone. I want to be connected to someone who values me. I want to feel like a person again and not a walking liability.

Christmas Eve

MY UNIT WILL DRIVE FROM FOB Summerall to FOB Speicher near Tikrit, Iraq. I drive a five-ton that won't shift out of third gear, stuck at 30 mph. We lose sight of the convoy that is going 55 mph. The sound of mortar rounds has plagued my deployment, as well as the thunder of IEDs (Improvised Explosive Devices) detonated by EOD squads or triggered by vehicles. I am expected to put vehicles back together again within twenty-four hours or maybe a week if the damage is bad. I am scared on this drive. My fear stems from the wreckage I've seen.

Once we reach Speicher I find the nearest MWR (Morale, Welfare, and Recreation program), where I wait for a computer to send an email to Amos, my fiancée. I met Amos after I left Germany and my unit was training at Fort Polk, Louisiana, at the JRTC (Joint Readiness Training Center). At the time, my unit was doing a training exercise and his unit was there as support. I was dirty and in need of a shower. Fortunately, through a mutual acquaintance, our paths crossed again, and we began dating.

Then I go back to my new quarters and wait. Four hours later I hear a knock, but it is just someone wanting to know if one of the other women wants to go to chow. I wait longer and write more letters. At 8 p.m., six hours after arriving, I am about to go to bed or find something to eat. As much as I want

Amos to find me, just knowing we are on the same base is reassuring. When I hear another knock, I open the door, ready to relay a message to an adjoining room.

Someone says, "Hi . . . it's me."

The overhang shadows his face and most of his body. I freeze. I know this voice. It is as if this voice awakens the part of me that's been hiding deep inside—the part I want to survive.

It's Amos. And I just hug him and cry. This is the worst and best Christmas Eve I have ever experienced.

We spend the rest of the evening together. I walk with him to my NCO's building and wait to ask for permission to spend Christmas with Amos and his unit. When he agrees, we go to each person on my chain of command and get further permissions. It is decided that on Christmas Day I will be signed out by Amos' lieutenant like a piece of equipment. I will be allowed to be out for the day and returned on Christmas evening.

Facing the Unknown

SIX WEEKS LATER I STAND in our building's bathroom. It is for pee-ONLY. In the middle of the night, I can go there without needing to wake someone up to walk with me to the closest porta potty. As a woman in the military, the chance of me being raped or assaulted is one in five. Taking a buddy with me to the outdoor potty is a safety precaution. Going alone to this bathroom is a luxury I didn't know I have missed.

I follow the directions and wait. The moment the lines cross, my heart drops, my mind races. I am awash with emotion. It is as if the world is muted. Questions of how this result will change my life overtake me.

I curse my unit's belief that birth control is only for those who are sluts to begin with. We female soldiers are not supposed to have sex, so why would we need it? Pregnancy is a scarlet letter in the military's book. Multi-National Iraqi forces have something called General Order Number 1, a five-page list of prohibited activities for soldiers. Before deployment we were all given copies, briefed, and quizzed. Among other things, the Order says anyone pregnant will be redeployed and single soldiers of the opposite sex are prohibited from spending the night together in any building.

The colonel who addressed my Brigade a few weeks before we deployed to Iraq went over General Order Number 1 with us. He warned that females would open their legs and tie a mattress to their backs to get out of deployment. Some, he said, want to be used like wheelbarrows.

A *deployment dodger,* I knew I wouldn't be that, and yet here I am, pregnant. I worry this is something else my unit will use to prove a point: females aren't cut out for deployments. Though I am Pro-Choice, I feel like I have no choices. I am a woman in Iraq where there are no abortions and my unit doesn't believe in providing birth control. Telling my commanding officer about my pregnancy may get me kicked out of the Army, with no honorable discharge, no veteran benefits.

Reality sets in with a loud knocking on the door. Someone else needs to use the bathroom. I go into my room and skip breakfast. I hide the test in my pocket. It feels like a lead weight. I feel like a traitor. But with each step I prepare myself for the fight I will be undertaking.

First, I will need to tell Amos. After that, I'll have to tell my unit. That will mean a trip to the medic to get the official results. I'm facing the unknown. Until now, I have never felt on the wrong side of the rules.

* * *

Amos was thrilled with my news. Our friends were happy. I was scared. I was going to wait one more day to tell my unit. Once I received a Pregnancy Profile I would be legally required to inform my unit of my condition, so they could get me out of the country within two weeks.

When I informed my NCO, it was right before he was to go on his two-week mid-tour leave, his R & R. He said two other NCOs wanted to help me. But he didn't know they were the same two sergeants who told me I was a disappointment to the unit when I had my breakdown at Summeral.

I was summoned to my Unit's HQ, a small, dingy building where additional weapons were locked away. Here we had a TV that was always on AFN-News, which was really CNN, and a radio tuned to the same frequency as other radios on the base. I had to present an official reporting to the commander and first sergeant. Our motor sergeant, who accompanied me to the Unit HQ, went in first to talk with the officers.

When the door opened, one of the officers motioned for me to go in. When they started by reading me my Miranda Rights, I knew. . . .

They saw me as a deployment dodger.

* * *

My new worksite was in the HQ, under the watchful eye of the senior command. I heard men talk about how soft the army had gotten, how women of other cultures will work until they go into the tree line and come out with a baby. They said DDs (Deployment Dodgers) got special treatment and made more work for everyone.

A day later I was called to report to the HQ Brigade, to the colonel. This time a different NCO from my motor pool accompanied me. This time first sergeants and captains from all units that were of mixed gender were in the room. I reported as I had done before. With formalities in place, I was once again read my Rights.

No, I was not raped.

Yes, I am pregnant, and I let my unit know after I went to the clinic.

Yes, I am aware of General Order Number 1.

No, I will not tell you the name of the father.

Yes, I do know who the father is.

NO, there is ONLY one.

No, birth control was not offered to me or any female in my unit.

Yes, I had a valid birth control prescription when I left for Iraq.

Yes, I did pack it.

Yes, I was at the pre-deployment briefing.

No, I am not under distress of retaliation from the father.

I want a lawyer.

I want a lawyer.

I WILL NOT ACCEPT OR SIGN THIS FIELD GRADE ARTICLE 15 (non-judicial punishment).

I WANT TO BE COURT MARTIALLED.

I WANT A LAWYER.

* * *

At night I would place my hands on my belly and talk to this small cluster of cells.

I would feel the immense pressure others must feel when an unexpected pregnancy comes.

Now I knew how a choice could change your life.

A Pebble in Their Boots

I LEFT IRAQ TO ENTER a new kind of battle. No mortars from the sky. No vehicles hit by improvised explosives. Back in my Rear Detachment Brigade at Ft. Campbell, adversaries who saw me as a deployment dodger confronted me.

Within the first week, someone from my Brigade tried to go with me to my initial OB/GYN appointment, actually tried to sit in the examining room. Some of the other pregnant women didn't know they could say no like I did. I understood it went against HIPPA.

I was given odd hours to report to my unit, sometimes three hours before everyone else came for the same formation. After they called me a liar when I complained, I started signing-in on the Brigade's twenty-four-hour guard roster.

In Iraq, I had lost sixty pounds within one five-month period. Still losing weight, I was labeled a Mild to High-Risk Pregnancy at fourteen weeks. The stress I was under plus severe morning sickness was taking its toll, not only physically but psychologically as well. I was put on a Special Pregnancy Profile that limited my activity further. When my doctor said I could not lift more than twenty pounds, the guys started weighing the boxes they wanted me to carry from one building to the next, to ensure they were at the maximum limit.

At sixteen weeks, I was hospitalized for spotting and bleeding. I had a partial placental abruption and spent three days in the hospital. While I was there, my unit commander and acting first sergeant came to accuse me of malingering. They said I was conspiring with the doctors to draw out the process and thus avoid getting kicked out of the military.

Upon my release, I was put on ten-day bed rest. After that I was to fulfill my daily fitness requirement by swimming rather than walking. Now I was bumped into HIGH Risk and was on a limited workday that began with swimming and didn't end for eight hours.

With all the pressure I was under and harassment, I was usually close to crying and turning into a puddle of mush. I felt depressed and wished my closest family support wasn't six hours away in Indiana. I began to see a mental health counselor and to make friends with other pregnant women in my fitness program.

* * *

June finally came around, and I picked up Amos at the Nashville airport on the tenth. He would be home for two weeks. I was relieved. My OB had me on six-hour workdays starting with swimming at 6:30 a.m. I could be home with Amos by one o'clock each afternoon. Even now I can't find the words to explain how it felt to be with someone who cherished me after weeks of enduring psychological torment and verbal disdain.

At 10 a.m. on June 17, I stood in Indiana, at the edge of a garden. Grandpa O'Neal escorted me down the aisle. I was happy for the first time since Christmas Eve. Once Amos and I were married I could loudly and proudly proclaim my husband was the father of the child in my womb.

My bliss was short-lived since Amos had to go back to Iraq. But now he carried a copy of our marriage license and wedding pictures. For the first time, he could say he was going to be a dad and not face persecution from his command. Unbeknown to me until this point was that my unit was working with his to try to bully him into confessing that he was the father. The plan against me would only work if they could get that confession. Just as they read me my Rights, they had done that to him.

* * *

It didn't take long for my unit to get back into the swing of things—their attempt to force me to my limits. I was again carrying boxes at my max weight. Once again I started bleeding and returned to the hospital. My placenta had started to tear again, so I was put back on bed rest for a week. Yet during that week I was escorted to a mental health appointment to see whether I was mentally sound enough to undergo Chapter 14: discharge from duty for misconduct proceedings. They wanted to charge me with Article 92: dereliction of duty, of willfully incapacitating myself by getting pregnant. I was deemed mentally sound and able to comprehend the charges against me as well as my legal rights. My paperwork also mentioned that, if the Chapter 14 didn't work, they recommended chaptering me out of the army for "depression and other mental health issues." I only received this paperwork later in my struggle.

On July 18 my lawyer filed Article 138 of the Uniform Code of Military Justice. This article gives any member of the armed forces who believes himself or herself wronged by a commanding officer the right to request redress. My lawyer had me obtain letters from all of my doctors to establish that I was under distress and needed to stay in the army for continuity of care.

* * *

My Rear Command now understood how serious I was about not letting them push me around and force me out. They responded to my Article 138, but not in the manner my lawyer and I had expected. Point by point, they explained why they did this or that and added sworn statements against me. There were statements from women who had bunked with me in Iraq and from soldiers I knew through the motor pool. Meaningless chit-chat was stretched out of context to paint me as a guilty party. Didn't most soldiers want to go home and forget what the Iraqi War had done to them? Didn't they also look forward to starting a family and finding happiness? When I responded to slanderous statements, my rebuttals were attacked.

I went to seek legal counsel to not only get my own copies of the files but to also seek my own character references. I filed another series of requests for Congressional inquiries as well as UCMJ (United States Code of Military Justice) complaints against my command.

On July 31 I knew the case my unit was trying to build against me was a sandcastle with high tide approaching. Trial Defense sent me a memorandum asserting it was unconstitutional for the military to ban sex between two single consenting adults. Trial Defense said my unit had no grounds for prosecution, and it would not process any such action if my unit tried to push the case further.

I was vindicated. I did nothing wrong. Now my battle was to get back on the promotion list so I might get E-5 benefits before I had my baby. Unfortunately, that didn't happen, but at least the pressure was off. All the pending actions against me were falling to the side. On August 29 I dropped my Article 138.

*   *   *

Throughout this time I also suffered from what I now know was PTSD, a condition caused by an experience in Iraq—a day of intense mortaring, when walls shook and two soldiers died. On July 4, 2006, I curled up on my bathroom floor as firecrackers exploded outside. I couldn't tell anyone, not even my doctors. I was in denial about what happened that day in Iraq and still can only speak of it obliquely.

That Day

Do not ask me what I know of war, of my time there, my *experience*.
    I can quote you the facts, the places and things my job entailed.
    I will give you a peek, but do not ask at what point I was lost,
    where I have struggled to return from.
    I can't, I can't, I can't.
        There are no words, only my raw senses grabbing
    bits of things. It hurts.
        I am still trying to piece it all together, make sense of
    the moment that haunts me and can consume me.
        I try to find a way to heal, with pills, therapy, and getting it
down, so I can logically see it as it was, not just feel it
over and over. Fuck you for wanting me to pin-point the moment.
    It's all the moment.
    It's all a blur. I will cry. I will go distant.
    If you prod me for more I will go back there and its weight
will bear me down. Recovery is a long road, and I have been on it
for such a long time.
    Half of me, the best part, is lost in Iraq. It's the part I wish I had
    for my children. So they could know who I was before *That Day*.

    I want so badly to have the trust and ignorance of those
who never go to war or send someone they love. I want their blind
faith in the system they support.
Did I break enough for you to know that I did experience it—
war, the dirty thing no one really wins?

I am lost in the rattling of the building, hours of mortars with no aim
other than us. I feel the dirt and sand in my eyes, try to rub it out
in my sleep ten years later. It wakes me up. I feel the earth move.
I see the craters of past attacks on my walks. Even now, every hole,
each indention on a flat surface, morphs into a cheating of death.

I see dried blood on T-walls, smell the dust, feel myself
clench in expectation of the unexpected. There's no release.
I am still clenched, still BATTLE-READY, still on alert. I feel
complete disregard for life, any life . . . mine.

Now that I am home or at least miles and years away
from where I see myself, even now *That Day* ripples and overlaps
with this day, *any* day.
    The part of me that wanted to change the world and protect what
    I held dear dissolved into a primal need to survive.
    And that is what I feel shame for.
    I feel the pity of those who *really* went into battle.
Can you validate that my time *Over There* was for something?
Do you believe I was protected by barbwire and concrete?
In buildings someone before us took? War is about taking
what you want and looking at what you did to get it,
how you made others fear you. We are all exposed.

What is the answer you are looking for?
I knew I could die.
I wanted nothing more than to live.
    And every day I battle myself, searching for some light.
I don't want *That Day* to define me. I want to move on, to stop feeling it.
I am angry at myself for not being okay with accepting my own death,
for wanting to take the life I have now, to snuff out the past,
    That Day. I feel shame that I am glad I wasn't killed.
    And shame that those who died felt it was worth it
    while I don't. The War isn't worth it.
    It has not been grounded on a worthy cause.
        I feel shame because until *That Day* and that moment,
I thought it was for a greater good. That my death would be more
than an ache in a mother's heart.
I feel anger, rage, frustration, and invisible.

I feel shame
I feel disappointment
I feel loss
I feel alone
I feel forgotten
I feel like I did die
      and the shell of me is a memory of my best parts.
      I am trying not to drown in this bleakness
      where pitch-black waves
            grab and pull me down.
How dare you ask me how *That Day, That Moment* impacts my life
and to what *intensity*. Screw You
for telling me you have other people coming in, *true* trauma victims
and survivors. FUCK YOUR IMPLICATIONS of priority,
      of what battle and war are to you.
      I was sent. I did my job, dammit,
      to Hell and back. I was in the Army.
      I went to Iraq. I saw death and mangled vehicles.
      I saw that it's easier to hate, to retaliate,
      to kill what makes us different.

      An eye for an eye.
      Bomb them.
      Shock and Awe.

      Nation Building—what a joke. It's *rape/pillage/plunder.*
I still don't have the words.
      I still can't
      tell you. Every time I try, I slip, I fall, I am overtaken.
      It was all for a lie.
      I was there and it changed nothing but me.

      That DAY... That Moment . . . That Blur of time on constant loop

Birth and Rebirth

I carry my light inside me, heavy like the harvest
that summer's abundance brings.

The light helps me not fade into darkness.
When ripples of battles ebb and flow,
I have my light transforming me
Into mother, each moment and each one after.
It knows my heartbeat from the inside
And shares my blood.
I give birth to my light and find
Joy in its movement. I bear witness
To my child, my light, a reason to fight and hope.

Purpose Redefined

MY DAUGHTER WAS BORN ON September 30 by emergency C-section due to fetal distress from all the placental abruptions during pregnancy. I had a few seizures on the table, causing me to lose about four pints of blood. My mother was there with me in the operating room. She cut the cord. She held my daughter the first four hours when I couldn't.

Five days after our daughter was born, Amos arrived home. My daughter and I were at his welcome home ceremony where he won a coin for having the youngest child there. Maternity leave went well, and our family life was blissful.

I wish this was the end of the story. Sadly, I still had to gather my resources. I refused to sell my leave time and be pushed out. IG, Legal Defense, and my lawyer helped me to receive all the leave I had earned. I ended up Out Processing from the Army and the 101st. My daughter was with me every step of the way. After all, she was with me as I fought the battle for Honorable Discharge and for my record to be cleared. For the record: to this day, only three people who I deployed with have talked to me. I have kept every piece of paperwork about this ordeal.

Now as a veteran, I am a warrior who has been a force for change. I can advocate and be the voice others don't have. I will fall, but I will learn from that and stand up again.

Booted

We have become scattered and separated,
grown dusty, hardened, and unacknowledged.
We are a silent monument to the other,
discarded for newer styles, lost in the closet
of stigma, misplaced with information mixed with lies.
I have lost what I clung to. I am amputated.

But my soul expands—the way air fills lungs,
burning from holding their breath—and I lace them up,
we come together, marching back
to become a pair, side by side, a testament
to our service. Ready to be called upon again
for our veterans deserve to not be forgotten
and discarded. The fight against injustice
is our motivation. My strong boots carry me.
Tested, they grow more creased, more capable.

Julia Snyder Whitehead began preparing for the Marine Corps as a sophomore at the University of South Carolina in 1992. Following Officer Candidate School in 1993, at the age of twenty-one, she was on active duty from 1994-1996 and left the service with the rank of lieutenant, homebased at Marine Corps Base Quantico, Virginia.

ONCE A MARINE, ALWAYS A MARINE

JULIA WHITEHEAD

To My Combat Boots
Someone else broke you in, softened you. . . .
You did not take to me, though,
Too big in the heel
Too small in the toe.
You were there early on
When the Major told Mom
The Marine Corps would take the smile
Out of my eyes.
It was almost true . . . almost.
On Cardiac Hill, you turned my toenails black
But guess what?
They grew back!
I couldn't stand the sight of you sometimes
But, boy, could you clean up.
I never told you, but I loved you
More than the pumps.
Dress shoes and dress blues are for grooms
And new-school generals, but you . . .
You were so strong, so durable.
Maybe you were like me back then
Not wanting to be broken.

South of the Border

SOUTH OF THE BORDER, IF you've not experienced that piece of Americana, is a little travel exit off I-95 in a place called Hamer, South Carolina. It is meant to resemble a kitschy Mexican town, with a large statue of "Pedro" in his sombrero. Billboards all along the interstate, starting in New Jersey or maybe further north, say things like: "You never sausage a place!" While these billboards will rightfully change in later years to remove the offensive stereotyping of Mexican Americans, at this time in the 1990s, these billboards are landmarks that provide a little bit of comic relief for me during a difficult drive. I imagine any drive is difficult for someone learning of a parent's death.

"Don't forget your Dress Blues," Mom had said over a scratchy phone line as I packed for Dad's funeral. Today, I am not driving to my childhood home in Indiana directly from Quantico, Virginia, where I've been on active duty in the Marine Corps for two months. I will make a pit stop first . . . a little detour to South Carolina, to tell my brother John about Dad's death because I don't want him to find out about it from one of his prison guards. And I won't tell him that Dad died on his birthday. That bit of news might break him more than the guards and prisoners at the South Carolina prison have broken him.

My brother John, age twenty-six, claimed he was armed when he tried to rob the gas station for drug money back before he was clean and sober. He thought that if he said he was armed he had a better chance of getting the clerk to give him the cash in the register. Of course, John wasn't armed. I remember John at age twelve, putting down his Red Rider BB gun after killing his first bird. He hadn't known what it was like to kill before that, and killing the bird was all it took for him to turn against guns. He wouldn't have hurt anyone. But when he spoke to a gas station clerk with an addict's mind, it didn't occur to him that pretending to have a weapon was psychologically as bad as actually having one. So he got five years in a South Carolina prison. And while I know it is fair and just that he receives that time in prison, I also know John. I also love John. His experience gives me an opportunity to expand my knowledge into this horrible microcosm of American culture . . . the prison system.

And it's hard not to think of the horrors of prison life as I'm driving on I-95. Impeccably timed, a South of the Border sign appears: "Road's scholar!" I giggle. These are hard years, the twenties . . . we are expected to be adults, but we don't have all the right skills yet. So many temptations . . . but one wrong move affects your future chances for greatness. I want to be valued and remembered by good people. When you go into the Marine Corps, you know there's the possibility that you could die at a young age. Why would I choose this when my friends are going to grad school or getting married or getting a regular job like bookkeeper or IT support person?

Did I choose the military because of Tyler? Dear Tyler . . . a great friend in high school and at the University of South Carolina . . . my friendly academic competitor who later turned to drugs in college and gave up on homework. With failing grades, Tyler's new plan was to join the Marines at the end of our freshman year of college. He committed suicide before that could happen. He took a gun into his college dorm room and shot himself. I was with him earlier that day. He said he needed to get a scientific calculator from his mom's house so I drove him home where he asked me to stay in the car as he went inside. I didn't know he was putting a gun into his bag. I didn't know anything about "manic depression" as it was called then or even depression. I didn't know his mother had walked in on him as he was holding a gun to his head the previous summer. I just knew he was one of my best friends who had it all together in high school and then made a downward spiral in college.

And later that night when I saw police cars outside his dorm, I was about to learn something new. . . . Those who commit suicide give their loved ones a lifetime of guilt when they depart the planet. And although counselors and others tell you it's not your fault, there's always a feeling that you could have done something to help. Something. Anything. Did I join the Marines to fulfill Tyler's plan for himself? Did I feel that guilty about not recognizing the signs of potential suicide? Or did I just want to get away from all of our friends, all of the suffering?

Maybe I joined the Marine Corps because of Dad, a funny, kind, and wise progressive patriot . . . the only kind of patriot I could ever stand to be around for very long. Dad . . . the World War II veteran. He was a small-town boy who raised me to believe I could have any career I wanted if I worked hard enough. He was someone who appreciated the brotherhood of man, a regular Kurt Vonnegut. Someone who could celebrate the Fourth of July and appreciate that Americans had certain special freedoms that are worth celebrating while always having in the back of his mind the recognition that nationalism is incredibly dangerous to humanity and should be kept in check. So much of what I am relates to Dad believing in me and encouraging me.

Or maybe I joined the military because of my big brother John, who, instead of graduating from high school, graduated from basic training from the Army base at Fort Leonard Wood, Missouri, later to be honorably discharged because he supposedly "could not learn." This, of course, was long before John ended up making a decision that landed him in prison. Later in life, I discovered that his learning disability had been identified and reported by one of his elementary school teachers, but no one bothered to do anything to try to address it in the 1970s and '80s. When he graduated from Army Basic Training, I was impressed with the discipline instilled in him. I was impressed with the idea of accomplishing goals, achieving the mission.

Or maybe I joined the military because of Mom and her work ethic, her pride in her brother Louis, missing in action . . . lost over the Atlantic during World War II on his flight from Brazil to North Africa. I feel a connection to this uncle I never met, Louis, who gave his life for something very important.

"Pedro's Weather Report: Chili today, Hot Tamale!" Again, I giggle. There are 120 South of the Border billboards on I-95. But as I wait to be buzzed in the visitor door at the prison to tell John of Dad's death, I don't know this. I just know that life is really hard sometimes, but, like the platoon commander says to us when we are on "a little walk in the woods" with our heavy packs and rifles: "Just put one foot in front of the other . . . That's all you have to do. . . . Take one step forward."

Training a Killer

TO BE A MARINE CORPS officer, you complete a summer of Officer Candidate School in Quantico, Virginia. This is an incredibly difficult training program designed to eventually create leaders of Marines. Since I was on a "reserve" commission, the military didn't pay for my education. After graduating from Officer Candidate School and college, I went through six months of The Basic School, which is anything but basic.

This introduction to basic infantry training is designed to show every Marine what it's like to be a "leatherneck" or, as some would say, a "grunt" and leader of grunts. This is where you become physically strong and lean. You learn to carry someone twice your weight. You hike from five to twenty miles on any given day with your heavy pack, rifle, and canteens. You spend hours learning how to navigate the woods with a map and compass.

This is where you learn about strategies and tactics. You jump from the high-dive with your pack and pretend to survive a burning oil slick in the water. You practice saying *no* to the villagers who try to board the helicopter as you are *evacuating a country.*

This is a competitive environment where your future career is determined by your performance unless you've been pre-qualified as a lawyer or pilot. You learn why General Lee won the Battle of Chancellorsville during the Civil War and why Lincoln's generals ultimately won the war. This is where you call for artillery fire to weaken the enemy and adjust the call for fire that you just made to perfect the location of the target, the people you want to destroy. You learn to throw a hand grenade and to take off your gas mask when ordered during a simulated chemical warfare attack. You learn a moment of the horror of chemical warfare.

This is where you pick ticks, those pesky little flat bugs, off your body as they manage to get into every fold and crevice of your skin . . . dozens of them . . . dozens of bugs that can cause Lyme Disease if you or your "buddy" aren't able to pick them off before they burrow under your skin. And, in my particular case, this is where I counted seventy-three ticks on my body in one outing.

This is where I destroyed my knees requiring me to later have two knee surgeries and then be told the next step is total knee replacement. This is where I had a noncancerous lump removed from my back only to find that the scar tissue created a larger lump that would become irritated when hiking with my pack. This is where I was too afraid to mention that I didn't have my earplugs on the rifle range because a potential loss of hearing seemed like a better alternative than being recognized as someone who forgot something. This is where I learned that the predator wolf is often knowingly placed in charge of the sheep, and that's a problem for the sheep. This is where I learned the most qualified and honorable men could sometimes be discarded if it benefits a higher-ranking person's ego.

This was peacetime.

This is also where I made at least one lifelong friend, a true friend. I discovered how incredibly strong my body could become. I learned the value of hard work and attention to detail. I learned that at any time in my life, I could say *"Semper Fi"* to a stranger who happens to be a Marine, and we both immediately know we will help each other accomplish any goal.

This is where I learned, that for all of my complaining about the Marine Corps, being a Marine Officer was one of the most significant accomplishments of my life. And when the Marine Hymn is played anytime, anywhere, I stand at attention and reflect on the institution . . . on people like Smedley Butler and other great leaders of past Marines. Smedley Butler wrote a book called *War Is a Racket,* which criticizes those government and corporate leaders who send our young ones off to war for commercial gain.

And I realize that being conflicted about military service is something for thinking people. Thinking people should be conflicted at times about this type of service. It is when people are not conflicted that they blindly follow instruction and violate Geneva Conventions and rights established for fighting men and women.

But the basic thing I learned at The Basic School always comes back to this: I learned to be a trained killer.

Conflicted

I PLAYED THE ROLE OF trained killer to the point that when it came time for us to compete with other Marines in a pugil stick competition, I was so much in the role that I saw my competitor as an enemy even though it was a training activity. I had her down on the ground . . . beaten . . . but I didn't stop there, even though that was technically the end of our bout. No. I chose to add insult to injury. I chose to cater to my bloodthirsty platoon that was cheering me on . . . men who loved watching two women fight each other. Two best friends. Two best friends who happened to have the same last name, the same Midwestern roots, nearly the same pattern of freckles on their faces.

My platoon cheered and cheered. I was dominating. I was victorious. I had served my platoon well. But when the captain finally pulled me away from her, she took off her helmet and I saw a new look in her eyes. She wasn't physically hurt, but her pride was hurt. I hoped she would forgive me for the unnecessary added embarrassment I caused her in front of her platoon. But that was not to be. Things were going to change. I learned that if women don't stick together in the military, then they could become the worst of enemies. Sometimes it's easier to be a member of the Brotherhood than a member of the Sisterhood. She looked at me as if I had the eyes of those Russians or those Libyans or those Iraqis that we sang about on our runs.

It was during that period of my Marine Corps training that I realized I was becoming a trained killer. Isn't that what I signed up for? But it didn't feel good to hurt another individual, whether it was their body or their pride. It didn't feel good to me. I couldn't bounce back from the way I treated my friend. I was conflicted inside. I wrote about it. I wrote in my journal that I had made a mistake by joining the military. I didn't want to be involved with hurting anyone, even in an indirect way. I knew what it was like to lose people I loved. I didn't want to be responsible for some other human losing a loved one.

I was playing the role of trained killer today, but what if in the future I played the role of an editor or a writer? A community volunteer? A teacher? A science writer? A museum director? A wife? A mother?

Gatekeeper of History

PUSHING ASIDE THE EMOTIONAL TRAUMA I'd been facing, I stepped through the doors of my work assignment—the Archives at the Marine Corps Research Center. Shelves of books stood in the archives, but the focal point of the public space was a large desk in front of a wall with a door that opened into the room where everything happened. I was the friendly, helpful person who sat at that desk and worked with other Marines to accomplish goals put forth by the Marine Corps History Center.

Some visitors to the archives were family members of Marines who passed away, relatives donating personal papers and artifacts to the University. Others were graduate students researching topics for required essays and other kinds of papers. The graduate students were from three different Marine Corps programs through which attendees could receive accredited courses and eventually masters degrees at Marine Corps University to advance their education and put them in a better place for promotion. Among other things, the archives had command chronologies, personal papers, a host of historical documents, and special collections.

I ensured that graduate students and other researchers would receive requested documents stored in the archives. Some Marines were in search of random and obscure facts, and I was the one who helped them solve the puzzle. It was a perfect gig for a nerdy, bookish Marine like me.

The archives was run by a civilian employee, a single woman with fifteen years at the organization and at least one cat in her home to match each year on the job. The archives was so rich in history that one day, when I walked in, I met a small group of reservists who had the task of shredding and archiving documents related to the first Gulf War. I was never allowed to go into one particular room, much like a vault, where these individuals spent days and days going through files, shredding who knows what, and organizing/cataloging other documents. They were not allowed to talk about their work.

Everybody had a different story. I met reservists assigned to shredding or archiving confidential paperwork, young Marines, going from this duty station to the next, doing a short stint at the archives, and Marines recovering from injuries who were transitioning back to work. I worked with civilians who had made this government job their career of choice as well as with high-ranking Marine officers in University administration who would come in and take part in planning activities. These were the people I grew to know during my last year in the Marine Corps. It was an atypical assignment.

I reported to a wonderful human being, Col. L. Messick. He taught me many things about the Marine Corps and gave me unique opportunities. One of these opportunities was an assignment to help lead a national Marine Corps History conference at Marine Corps University. I was a glorified event planner who arranged hotel rooms for our key speakers, lined up food, structured the agenda for each day, set up the room and content, etc. With so much physically and mentally demanding training behind me, I was happy to have work that allowed me to be resourceful.

The day of this history conference proved influential to my eventual career path. When one attendee, Owen, a vice president of a division of Random House Publishing, thanked me for successfully planning and implementing the conference activities, I had no idea he would become my next supervisor as I transitioned from the Marine Corps to a full-time job with his company. I am grateful to Col. Messick for encouraging me to follow up with the "guy from Random House" who left me his business card and suggested he might have a job opportunity for me.

While I can't say there was a "typical" day in the Archives, I can say that this experience, with all of its unique situations, gave me the confidence and skills I needed to later create the Kurt Vonnegut Memorial Library in Indianapolis. It offered me an environment much different from Officer Candidate School and The Basic School, where I had received the usual nationalistic propaganda and trained to be a killer. At the Marine Corps Research Center, I saw there were other "thinking people" in the Marine Corps, inquisitive readers and problem-solvers with interesting experiences to share.

My Inner Marine Makes Sense of It All

WHEN THE WRITING WORKSHOP FOR the creation of this book started, I was nervous about participating. I was scared to share my story with others. I didn't want to revisit past hurts, and I didn't want to revisit those hurtful things I did. While I don't reveal some of the most hurtful experiences of my military service in this book, I did share those hurts with my fellow women veterans. Interestingly, several of them had similar experiences. Talking about my experience with these women helps me to heal. We meet and will continue to meet as a supportive group of creative, extraordinary people.

For my section, I chose the title "Once a Marine, Always a Marine" for a number of reasons. Over the past twenty years, I had been trying to push myself as far away from my Marine Corps experience as I could get. This writing workshop has helped me realize that those years are a part of who I am. Most of the people I met in the military were people like me . . . people who just needed a job or young people who wanted to believe in something larger than themselves . . . a greater calling, a duty. Connecting with my fellow women veterans has helped me to make sense of my experience and put it in the overall framework of my life.

The writer and mythology/religion scholar Joseph Campbell talked about how one can look back on one's life and notice a pattern . . . a pattern that helps to make sense of it all. The pattern of my life would not have been complete without my service as a U.S. Marine. While there is no way to know for certain, I believe certain jobs would not have come my way without my service as a Marine Corps officer. My editing, writing, and publishing experience with Random House, Eli Lilly and Co., and the nonprofit Military Officers Association of America provided me with skills I called upon as I founded the Kurt Vonnegut Memorial Library, a museum/library dedicated to one of the key thinkers of the Twentieth Century.

My inner Marine is reflected in my early-morning wakeup to squeeze as much out of one day as I possibly can. Recognizing that life is short and can be cut short without notice, my inner Marine helps me to accomplish my life goals. My inner Marine tells me not to make excuses and to lead others to solutions.

My inner Marine gives me the strength to create something out of nothing. Time has not healed the wounds I suffered during my peacetime service in the military. But thanks to the creative writing process needed to make this book, I have come to realize that my life is richer. My various jobs have required me to write in a business voice, but helping to create *Finding the Words* showed me that I am also a creative writer. I have stories to tell, as do all of the courageous women whose work you are reading in this book. I am grateful to the Indiana Writers Center and to the staff and board of the Kurt Vonnegut Memorial Library for helping me locate and identify my inner Marine, for helping me make sense of it all.

Directionally Challenged No More

To a WWI compass found in an antique shop in the Tar Heel State, a graduation gift from Mom & Dad

On my last day at Marine Corps Officer Candidate School,
I became your owner for life.

You returned me to the South, where I love the azaleas
and hate the racial inequality.

You took me East, to live among the Bengali, the Vietnamese,
the Khmer, the Thai.
You said, *Go west, West, young woman,* to the red rocks,
the desert, the rugged coast, the purple mountain majesty.

But I was still looking for my place.

You pointed me North, back home again, to a Hoosier life,
the life I always wanted.

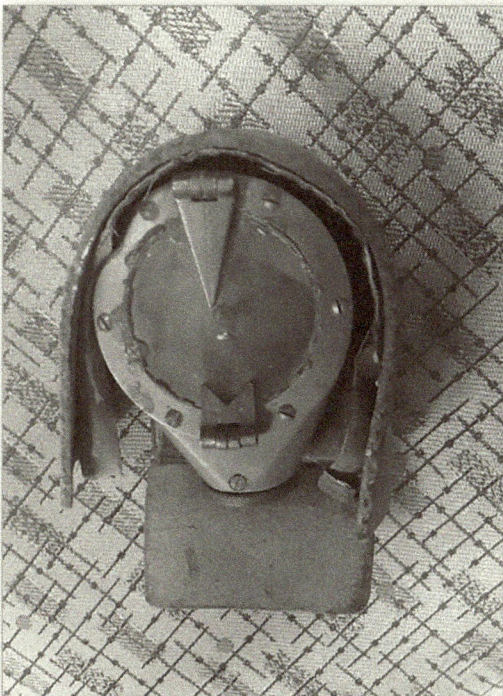

Glossary of Military Acronyms

1SGT: First Sergeant

ACU: Army Combat Uniform

AIT: Advanced Individual Training

ASVAB: Armed Services Vocational Aptitude Battery

AT: Annual Training

BC: Battalion Commander

BCT: Basic Combat Training or Boot camp

BDE: Brigade

BDU: Battle Dress Uniform

BOLC: Basic Officer Leadership Course

BSA: Brigade Support Area

CLP: Cleaner, Lubricant and Preservative

CLS: Combat Life Saver

CMT: Combat Medic Training

CPT: Captain

CSH: Combat Support Hospital

C5-A: Large Military Transport Aircraft

DC: Division Commander

DCU: Desert Camouflage Uniform

DFAS: Defense Finance and Accounting Service

DMZ: Demilitarized Zone

DOD: Department of Defense

DZ/LZ: Drop Zone/Landing Zone

EO: Equal Opportunity

EOD: Explosive ordinance disposal

ETS: End Term of Service

FOB: Forward Operating Base

GI: Government Issue (general term for someone in the military)

GIB: Guy in Back

HHC: Headquarters and Headquarters Company

HIK: Hickam Air Force Base, Hawaii

HUMINT: Human Intelligence

IED: Improvised Explosive Device

IET: Initial Entry Training

IG: Inspector General

INF: Infantry

KUV: Kunsan Air Base, South Korea

LBV: Load Bearing Vest

LMTV: Light Medium Tactical Vehicle

LN: Local National

LSA: Logistics Support Area

LT: Lieutenant

M16: Assault Rifle

MCWR: Marine Corps Women's Reserve

MEPS: Military Enlistment Personnel Station

MI: Military Intelligence

MOPP2: Mission Oriented Protective Posture, Level 2, gear for toxic exposure

MOS: Military Occupational Specialties

MOUT: Military Operations in Urban Terrain

MP: Military Police

MRE: Meal Ready to Eat

MSR: Main Supply Route

MST: Military Sexual Trauma

NASA: National Aeronautics and Space Administration

NCO: Non-Commissioned Officer

NVG: Night Vision Goggles

OCS: Officer Candidate School

OFC: Officer

OJT: On-the-Job Training

OKO: Yokota Air Base, Japan

OP: Operations Post

OPFOR: Opposing force

OPORD: Operation Order

PID: Positive Identification

PFC: Private First Class

PMCS: Preventative Maintenance Checks and Services

PT: Physical training

PVT: Private

QRF: Quick Reaction Force

ROE: Rules of Engagement

RTD: Return to Duty

SAW: Squad Automatic Weapon

SECFOR: Security Force

SERE: Survival, Evasion, Resistance, and Escape Training

SFC: Sergeant First Class

SGT: Sergeant

SPC: Specialist

SSG: Staff Sergeant

STB: Special Troops Battalion

SUU: Travis Air Force Base, California

TOC: Tactical Operations Center

TSC: Tactical Support Center

USAF: United States Air Force

USAF E5: Staff Sergeant

USO: United Service Organization (Supports US Troops)

UXO: Unexploded Ordinance

VBIED: Vehicle-Borne Improvised Explosive Device

XO: Executive Officer

Writing Prompts

Prompt #1: Why I Enlisted

What particular event(s) led you to enlist? As you look further back, what formative forces also played a role in your decision?

The first part of the prompt asks you to describe influential events that occurred just prior to your decision to enlist. The latter part asks you to search further back, to think about where you are from. This might include a town, culture, time period, neighborhood, community, friends, and family. How did where you come from shape who you were as a young woman and your ideas of war and the military? How did it influence your choice to go into the service and what you carried with you?

Prompt #2: What I Learned in Boot Camp

Describe what you learned from your boot camp or training camp experience. You might focus on what the officers wanted you to learn or you might concentrate on other types of lessons you picked up. You could even write about what you didn't learn—or should have.

Prompt #3: Doing My Job

Show us what your job in the military was like. Help us understand what it was like being you and doing whatever your job was. What was an ordinary workday like? How was your job different from your expectations? What was it like being a woman doing your job?

Prompt #4: Crossing the Line

Write about a time in your military experience when you (or someone you knew) broke a rule, defied authority or acted against an expectation. Conversely, you might write about a time when you wanted to break a rule, defy authority, or act against an expectation but failed to do so.

Prompt #5: Being Female in the Military

What was it like being a female in the military? What was the culture like and how did it affect you? Did reality match or differ from your expectations? Did you challenge any sexual stereotypes? What happened?

Prompt #6: Where I Went

Where did you go during your time in the military? Describe one specific place that is particularly memorable for you in some way. This might be a base or camp, a battle site, a village or neighborhood, a place for recreation, a particular mountain, or a body of water.

Prompt #7: Someone I Met

Write a story or poem about someone you met through your military experience. What has been the significance of this relationship? What did you learn from it? Did it cause you to change the way you think or your actions?

Prompt #8: The Hardest Thing

What did you find most difficult about serving in the military? Was it facing danger? Taking part in violence? Coping with boredom? Being away from home? Eating the food? Learning another language? Dealing with sexism? Whatever this challenge was, describe it vividly through a story or series of anecdotes. Did this challenge teach you anything about yourself or human nature?

Prompt #9: A Gift

Write a story about a gift you received during your term of service. This gift could be from anyone—someone in your unit, a family member back home, a commander, civilian, even an enemy. Perhaps this gift didn't appear to be a gift at first.

Prompt #10: A Holiday

Focus on one memorable holiday you celebrated while in the service. This holiday might be unforgettable for how much fun it was or for how things went horribly wrong or for how it contrasted with the same holiday back home. Consider the significance of this event and its consequences.

Prompt #11: An Important Song

Was there a particular song or type of music that was important to you while you were in the service? Why was it important? Do you have any stories or anecdotes related to this song or type of music? Another option: Instead of focusing on music, explore the personal significance of a book you read or a movie you saw while in the service.

Prompt #12: Communicating with Loved Ones Back Home

Do you have a story or series of anecdotes related to the way you communicated with family or friends back home? Did email and Skyping make it harder or easier to serve away from home? Do you have any interesting stories related to care packages?

Prompt #13: Receiving (or Not Receiving) a Certain Distinction

Write about a distinction that you or someone close to you received or failed to receive. Consider why you wanted (or didn't want) this recognition or appointment. What did you do to try to get it (or not get it)? What were the after-effects? Focus on details that will create suspense.

Prompt #14: Description of an Object

Through a short prose piece or poem, explore an object from your military experience that has significance for you, perhaps in some way you don't even understand yet. It might be a photograph, journal, postcard, memento, piece of equipment, item of clothing, game, or food item.

Prompt #15: Going Home

What was it like going home after your military service? What did you carry back with you? How had you changed? Did you have to overcome any obstacles in order to feel at home again or find healing? Are you still overcoming obstacles? Would you enlist again if you had it all to do over again? What do you know now that you didn't know then?

Selected Readings

Ward Britt. "Bad Moon Rising" and "Staging Battalion" from *Returning: Stories from the Indianapolis Senior Center*

Jess Goodell. *Shade It Black: Death and After in Iraq*

Randall Jarrell. *The Complete Poems*

Shoshana Johnson. *I'm Still Standing: From Captive U.S. Soldier to Free Citizen—My Journey Home*

Yusef Komunyakaa. *Warhorses*

Heidi Squier Kraft. *Rule Number Two: Lessons I Learned in a Combat Hospital*

Tim O'Brien. *If I Die In a Combat Zone, Box Me Up and Ship Me Home*

Brian Turner. *Here, Bullet, Phantom Noise,* and *My Life as a Foreign Country*

Maxine Cardinal Wehry. *A Kindred Spirit*

Kayla Williams. *I Love My Rifle More Than You: Young and Female in the U.S. Army*

Tobias Wolff. *In Pharaoh's Army*

About the Writers

Leslie Bales

I became a Hoosier twenty-five years ago when my husband, a Chief Petty Officer with the U.S. Navy, was reassigned from serving aboard advanced attack nuclear submarines to working in Indianapolis. We made the move so that our two sons, Dustin and Derek, would have a father at home during their teenage years.

Serving those who serve has become a way of life for my family, most of whom work for the Defense Finance and Accounting Service (DFAS). My lengthy career as a civil servant allows me opportunities to influence change and mentor others to succeed in their careers. As a change leader, I implement technical solutions that improve business processes for the seven million servicemen and women DFAS serves.

In 2005, at age forty-five, I graduated with a Bachelor of Science degree in Management from Indiana Wesleyan. Twelve months later, after attending a resident program with the National Defense University in Washington, D.C., I earned a Masters in Information Management from Syracuse University.

I enjoy writing in the summer sun on our pontoon boat docked feet from my back deck. As I listen to fish jump and watch eagles soar, I'm inspired and the words flow. My greatest joys have been renovating our cabin and spending time at the lake with children and grandchildren.

Robin Hall

Growing up in Roxbury and Jamaica Plain, Massachusetts, allowed me to experience social, racial, and geographical diversity throughout my formative years. After graduating from Jamaica Plain High School, I attended Barrington College in Rhode Island to study Pre-Veterinary Medicine. Due to my athletic interests, I changed direction, receiving a BS in Physical Education. Later I received an MS in Physical Education/Athletic Training from Indiana State University. Other interests led me to courses in auto mechanics, HVAC (heating, ventilation, and air conditioning), and certification as both an EMT and Pharmacy Technician. In 2008 I completed a BS in Biology at Franklin College. My husband calls me a perpetual student.

I've worked as a veterinary technician, junior high and high school teacher and coach, camp counselor, service station manager, building maintenance employee, natural resource technician, and environmental specialist.

While in the military, I found the love of my life whom I've been married to for thirty-three years. I enjoy being part of his family of three grown children, fourteen grandchildren, and six great-grandchildren (so far).

My favorite things to do include hanging out with family and friends, hiking, backpacking, creating various forms of art, gardening, traveling, and learning about health and nutrition.

Cindy "Loc" Hornung

My Vocational Rehabilitation counselor, D. McCloud, suggested that, as
a Service Connected Veteran, I take an
online writing course through Gotham
Writers Workshop (GWW) to fulfill a
Life Skills program requirement. I chose
science fiction. I took two courses and
found that I enjoyed writing. My instructor, M. Roessner, encouraged a confidence in me that my writing presented a
certain "voice."

Fresh from my experience with GWW
and in pursuit of another, that of VA Peer
Specialist, I signed up for the Women
Veterans Memoir Workshop.

Laura McKee

As the Women Veterans Coordinator for the Indiana Department of Veterans Affairs, I serve as the advocate for all women veterans in the State of Indiana and promote women veterans awareness. I also review programs meeting the needs of these women and work to improve veteran benefits and services.

I serve as an Air Force Reservist with the 434th Air Refueling Wing at Grissom Air Reserve Base, Indiana. I'm an Assistant Chief Inflight Refueler with the 72nd Air Refueling Squadron. In the past twenty-six years, I have been deployed numerous times in support of operations, including Operation Iraqi and Enduring Freedom.

I earned a Bachelor's degree from Indiana University and also graduated from the Community College of the Air Force with two Associate of Applied Science degrees in Aviation Operation Aircraft Technology and Systems Maintenance Technology. My service history is filled with honor, dedication, and commitment beginning with Operation Desert Shield and Storm to the most recent Operation Inherent Freedom. I've been a lifelong resident of Indiana.

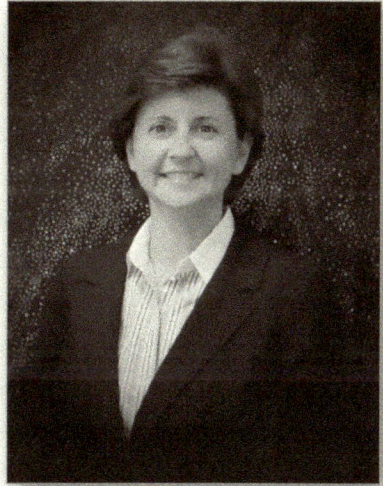

Shanna Reis

I grew up moving from state to state to keep up with my step-father's Navy career until middle school when my mother decided to settle down and told him to come back and visit when he got leave. Now years later we all still live in Indianapolis.

I received my BFA in Sculpture from Herron School of Art and Design after my second six-year contract with the Army was over and have just been accepted into a graduate program with an emphasis on printmaking. My plan is to combine my love of papermaking and poetry to make editions of art books. When I'm not being used as a couch for my dog or my little niece, I enjoy building "found" object sculptures and contemplating the possibilities of art in virtual reality.

Anita Hupy Siccardi

As a servant leader for over fifty-four years, I have combined my two passions: nursing and education. My education includes a bachelor's, two master's and a doctorate degree. During most of my career, I was raising three wonderful children. I have held positions in almost every role as a nurse and educator, including service as a captain in the Army Nurse Corps in Nuremberg, Germany, and in Saudi Arabia during Desert Storm. At the age of fifty, I made the decision to enlist based on the Army's need for nurses. Until retiring in the summer of 2016, I was the Dean of Nursing at Marion University Leighton School of Nursing in Indianapolis.

Elizabeth "Betty" Smith

After WWII I married former 1st Lt. Earl R. Smith who had served in the Signal Corps under General George Patton in Europe. My daughter Sharon was born in 1951. Throughout the years, I stayed in close contact with my three brothers and their families.

Earl and I retired in 1971 and purchased a thirty-two-foot Airstream Trailer and a new car to pull it. One month before we were to leave, Earl had a stroke but recovered in great fashion; however, he could not drive. I did the driving, and in the next five years we traveled 90,000 miles through this beautiful country.

In 1977 I became a widow. I traveled with three widow friends to Europe, the Greek Isles, and Australia. A working freighter ship took us around the world, and we were at sea for three-and-a-half months. I became a history buff, with particular interest in Egypt and Ancient Rome. In regards to reading, I prefer nonfiction to fiction.

In June 2016 I moved from Indianapolis into an independent living facility in Springfield, Missouri, where my daughter, grandson, and two great-grandchildren live. I lost my last brother in 2011.

Christylee Vickers

As a veteran, I do my best to advocate for other veterans, bringing awareness to such invisible injuries as PTSD, anxiety, and depression, all of which impact my life on a daily basis. I also parent a child with non-neurotypical needs, so I am always looking for ways to find balance in life. When things get bad, I seek out creative outlets to channel my negative energy into something constructive and expressive. I have crochet projects in various stages of completion, a sketchbook of ideas for paintings and sculptures, and notebooks with stories, poems, and the random grocery list. In the last few years, raising chickens has helped me focus on the present instead of Iraq.

My goal is to open an Artisan Farm/Retreat for veterans or veterans with their families, where they can spend time learning food sustainability practices, as well as such crafts as pottery, blacksmithing, and fiber arts. I want to help veterans and their families transition back to civilian life

I also want to walk the Appalachian Trail from start to finish, travel internationally, write some books, and exhibit the artwork I've created to help me work through major mood events, insomnia, or blocks in my logic. I can't change everything, but with the unwavering support of my husband Amos, I can do enough to instigate a ripple of positive change. For all veterans, the stigma of having mental health issues needs to end.

Julia Whitehead

I grew up in Northern Indiana. My father had served in World War II and was turning fifty when I was born. His first heart attack happened when I was four-years-old. Mom grew up on a farm and worked for Studebaker during World War II. When I came along as child number six, Mom ran an antique shop in our family home. With four brothers, I spent a lot of time playing sports or trying to tame baby snakes and turtles we'd find in Mom's garden.

We moved to South Carolina, where a southern belle called me a "carpetbagger" on the first day of ninth grade. In high school and at the University of South Carolina, I worked for a newspaper and later as a legislative aide to a state representative.

Following Marine Corps service, I worked for Random House publishers, and Military Officers Association of America while studying at George Washington University. I taught English in Thailand before returning to Indiana to work for the state legislature.

Extraordinary coincidences and decisions led to the birth of my son Daniel, my marriage to J.T. Whitehead, and the birth of our second child, Joseph. I worked for Eli Lilly and Co. and took night classes to get my master's degree before starting the Kurt Vonnegut Memorial Library in 2011. So it goes . . . .

Lisa Wilken

I currently reside in Indiana with my husband and two sons. Along with being a wife and mother, I volunteer my time to serve military and veterans in my local community. After leaving the Air Force, I worked in the lab field using my military training.

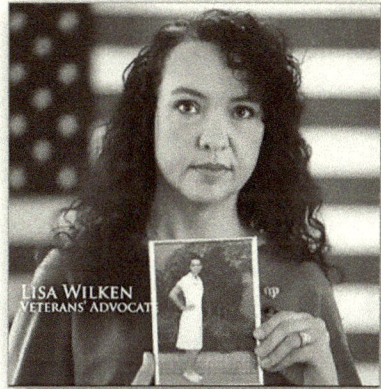

I am currently the Legislative Director for AMVETS, Department Indiana, an elected position, and have been appointed by the current and past Commander of AMVETS, Department Indiana, as their Women Veteran Liaison. I use my experience in the military and with the Department of Veterans Affairs to help other veterans and their families maneuver a sometimes difficult system.

About the Editors and Book Designer

Editor

Shari Wagner teaches poetry and memoir writing for the Indiana Writers Center. She is Indiana Poet Laureate for 2016-2017 and the author of two books of poems: *The Harmonist at Nightfall* and *Evening Chore*. She is also the co-author with her father of *A Hundred Camels* and *Making the Rounds: Memoir of a Small-Town Doctor* and editor of *Returning: Stories from the Indianapolis Senior Center*. Her work has appeared in *The Writer's Almanac, American Life in Poetry, Shenandoah,* and *North American Review*. (www.shariwagnerpoet.com)

Volunteer Editors

Patricia Cupp is a retired teacher who, through the Indiana Writers Center, has assisted with many memoir writing projects. She has worked with children and adults, helping them "find the words" for their amazing stories. She has recently published a collection of poems entitled *Dressing for the Weather*. She enjoys traveling and gardening. Working with the women veterans in this book has been an educational and rewarding experience.

Barbara McLaughlin is a journalist, novelist, and children's book author. She began her career in sports writing and traveled the world with U.S. Olympic and national diving teams. Her picture book, *Reuben Rides the Rails,* was a Christamore House selected book in 2010. A former Indiana Writers Center board member, she helped edit and contributed to the 2015 anthology, *Where Mercy and Truth Meet: Homeless Women of Wheeler Speak*. In her spare time, she enjoys running marathons and finds qualifying for Boston easier than getting her novels published.

Barbara Shoup is the author eight novels, including four for young adults, and the co-author of *Novel Ideas: Contemporary Authors Share the Creative Process*. She is the Executive Director of the Indiana Writers Center.

Carol Weiss has been a journalist and has co-authored three nonfiction books. She was presented the "Dorothy Riker Hoosier Historian Award" by the Indiana Historical Society in 2005. *Skirting the Issue: Stories of Indiana's Historical Women Artists,* co-authored with Judith Vale Newton, received numerous awards and honors. Currently Carol is president of the board of the Indiana Writers Center.

Book Designer

Andrea Boucher is currently earning her MFA in the Butler University Creative Writing Program. In addition to writing creative nonfiction and teaching classes at the Indiana Writers Center, she also freelances as a designer. She has done numerous cover and book designs for the IWC, including *Not Like the Rest of Us: An Anthology of Contemporary Indiana Writers; I Remember: Indianapolis Youth Write about Their Lives; Where Mercy and Truth Meet: Homeless Women of Wheeler Speak; Flying Island; Life Dances;* and two books in the Workshop Series, *Dream Workshop* and *Memory Workshop.*

ANITA SICCARDI

Captain Anita Hupy Siccardi goes into the field to invite tankers to the Camp Henry Talent Show.

SHANNA REIS

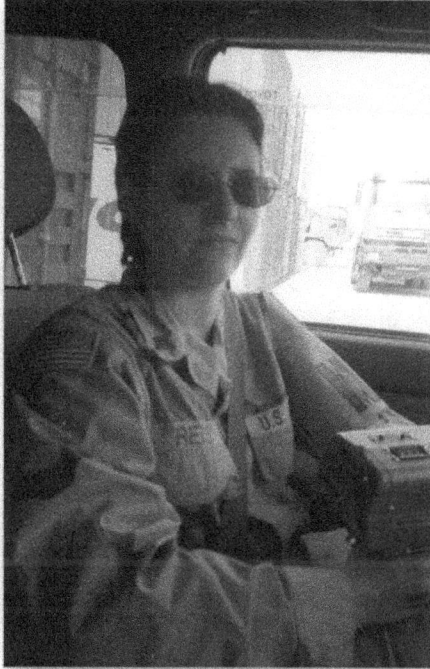

*Shanna Reis enforces speed limits at
Camp Phoenix, Afghanistan.*

ELIZABETH SMITH

Elizabeth Von Tobel Smith visits her brother Frances after his battleship, the USS West Virginia, is torpedoed by a Japanese submarine.

CINDY "LOC" HORNUNG

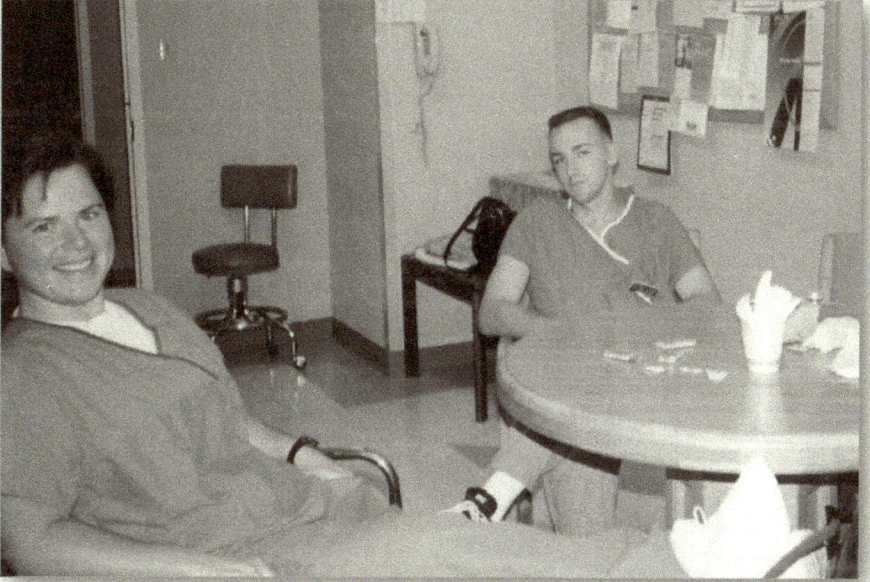

Cindy "Loc" Hornung takes a break during clinical rotations.

ROBIN HALL

Captain Robin Hall ready to participate in the Indianapolis 500 Festival Parade with the Indiana National Guard Ceremonial Unit Mounted Color Guard.

LAURA McKEE

*Laura McKee considers her uncle, PFC
Welden E. Bucher, one of her true
inspirations.*

LISA WILKEN

Lisa Wright Wilken and her roommate at Shepherd Air Force Base.

CHRISTYLEE VICKERS

Christylee Hawk Vickers spends time with her future husband, Amos, before being deployed to Iraq.

LESLIE BALES

Leslie Coats Bales and Theron "Ted" Coats stand outside the base chapel at Lackland AFB, April 1978.

JULIA WHITEHEAD

Julia Snyder Whitehead smiles while being tricked into digging up her hat.

224

Acknowledgments

Finding the Words is a creation of the Women Veterans Memoir Workshop,
one in a series of community-based memoir workshops conducted by the Indiana Writers Center (IWC) under the direction of its Executive Director, Barbara Shoup, and Education Outreach Director, Lyn Jones. The Workshop, which met for twelve sessions, from October 2015 to March 2016, was funded by the generosity of the Allen Whitehill Clowes Charitable Foundation, Inc.

I wish to thank Julia Whitehead, CEO and Founder of the Kurt Vonnegut Memorial Library (and a member of our workshop), for offering us the Vonnegut Library as a comfortable meeting place in downtown Indianapolis. Thanks, too, to Kate Newman, the Vonnegut Library's Community Relations Associate, who helped us with publicity and catered to our needs while in the library. Thanks to Katz & Korin, PC for workspace and assistance, to Foundry Provisions for donating savory coffee for every meeting, and to Marriott's Courtyard Indianapolis at the Capitol for providing us with convenient and complimentary parking.

Special thanks to author Kayla Williams for the review on our book's back cover. She is director of the VA's Center for Women Veterans, but her review was prepared in her personal capacity; the opinions expressed are her own and do not reflect the view of the Department of Veterans Affairs or the United States Government.

As I taught the workshop, I was extremely fortunate to have a team of deeply dedicated IWC volunteers assisting me. These women—Patricia Cupp, Barbara McLaughlin, and Carol Weiss—are all published writers who have assisted with other IWC outreach projects. They gave the veterans excellent feedback on their stories and poems and, along with Barbara Shoup, formed a wonderful editing team as the final copy was prepared. Special thanks to Patricia for her time in helping Betty Smith, our oldest veteran, write down her stories.

I'd also like to express my appreciation to Shanna Reis, a member of our workshop, for the powerful artwork on this book cover and to Andrea Boucher for her expert skills in designing this book's cover and layout.

Finally, I want to express my abiding gratitude and admiration for the authors of this book—the ten members of the Women Veterans Memoir Workshop. Thank you, ladies, for your commitment to the workshop and to this book, for your honesty, hard work, and the amazing support you've given to me and each other.

Shari Wagner
IWC Instructor

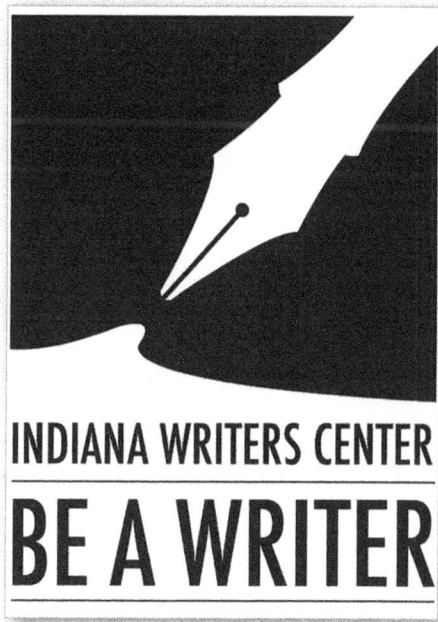

www.ingramcontent.com/pod-product-compliance
Lightning Source LLC
Chambersburg PA
CBHW020851090426
42736CB00008B/333